# Anne Frank

written by
**Joe Dunn**
illustrated by
**Ben Dunn**

magic
Wagon

## visit us at
## www.abdopublishing.com

Published by Magic Wagon, a division of the ABDO Publishing Group, 8000 West 78th Street, Edina, Minnesota 55439. Copyright © 2008 by Abdo Consulting Group, Inc. International copyrights reserved in all countries. All rights reserved. No part of this book may be reproduced in any form without written permission from the publisher. Graphic Planet™ is a trademark and logo of Magic Wagon.

Printed in the United States.

Written by Joe Dunn
Illustrated by Ben Dunn
Colored by Robby Bevard
Lettered by Joe Dunn
Edited by Stephanie Hedlund
Interior layout and design by Antarctic Press
Cover art by Rod Espinosa
Cover design by Neil Klinepier

### Library of Congress Cataloging-in-Publication Data

Dunn, Joeming W.
   Anne Frank / written by Joe Dunn; illustrated by Ben Dunn.
   p. cm. -- (Bio-graphics)
   Includes index.
   ISBN 978-1-60270-065-9
   1. Frank, Anne, 1929-1945--Juvenile literature. 2. Jews--Netherlands--Amsterdam--Biography --Juvenile literature. 3. Jewish children in the Holocaust--Netherlands--Amsterdam--Juvenile literature. 4. Amsterdam (Netherlands)--Biography--Juvenile literature. 5. Graphic novels. I. Dunn, Ben. II. Title.

DS135.N6F7329 2008
. 940.53'18092--dc22
 [B]                                       2007012064

# TABLE of CONTENTS

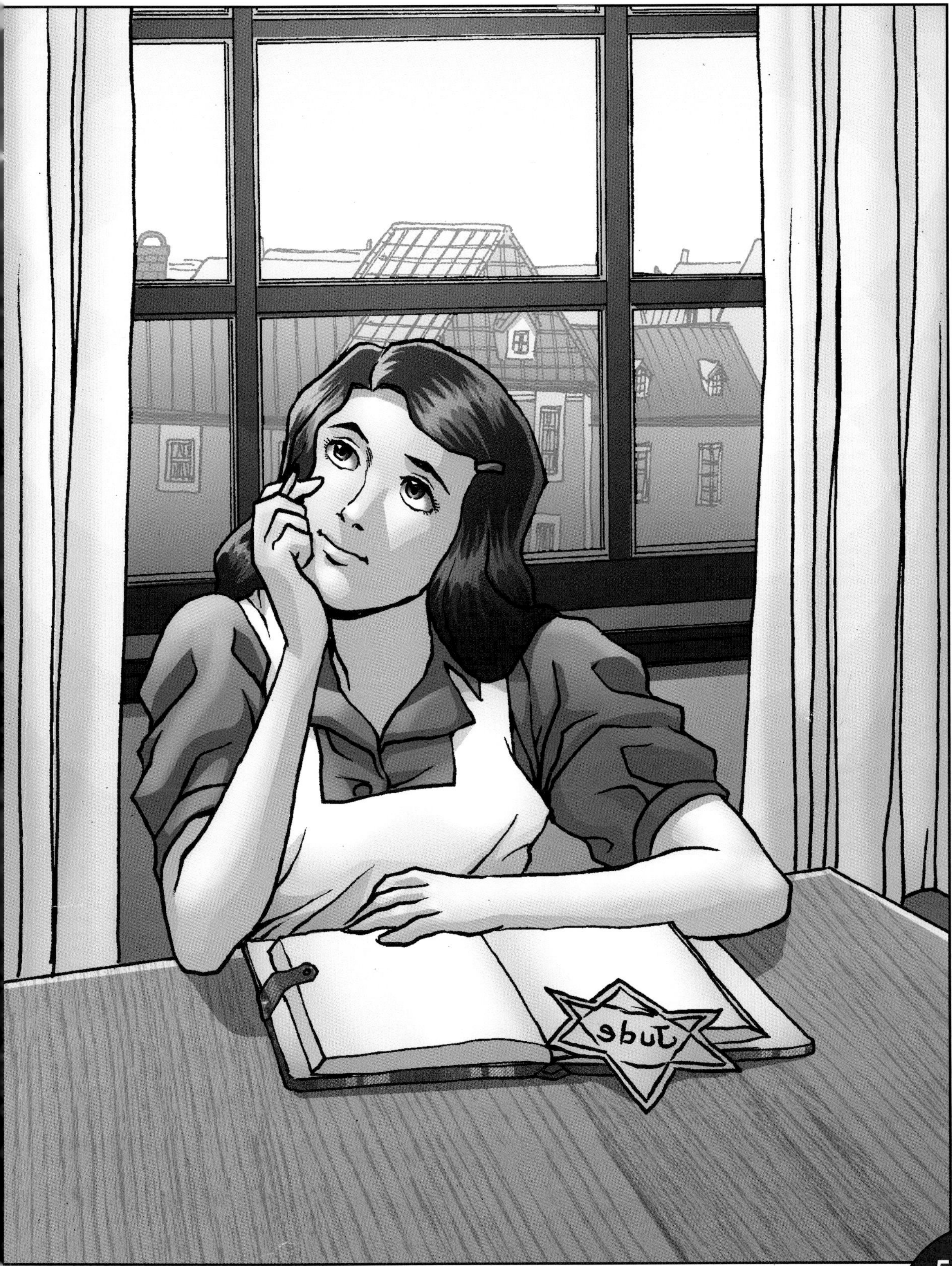
Jude

# Chapter 1 Life in Germany

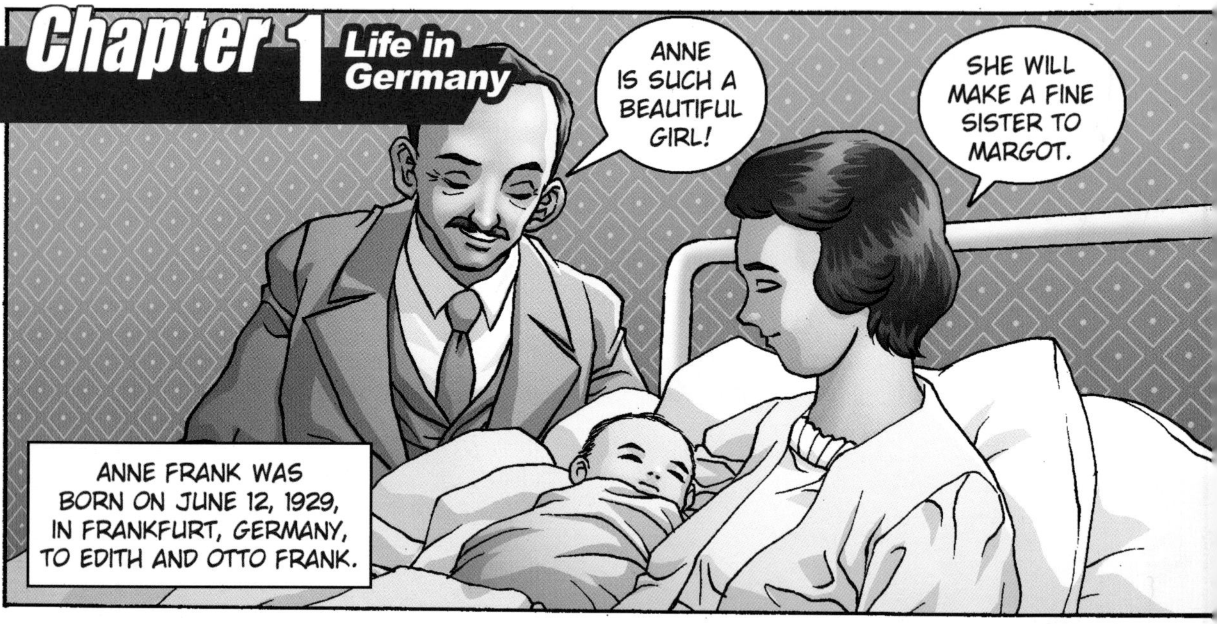
ANNE IS SUCH A BEAUTIFUL GIRL!
SHE WILL MAKE A FINE SISTER TO MARGOT.
ANNE FRANK WAS BORN ON JUNE 12, 1929, IN FRANKFURT, GERMANY, TO EDITH AND OTTO FRANK.

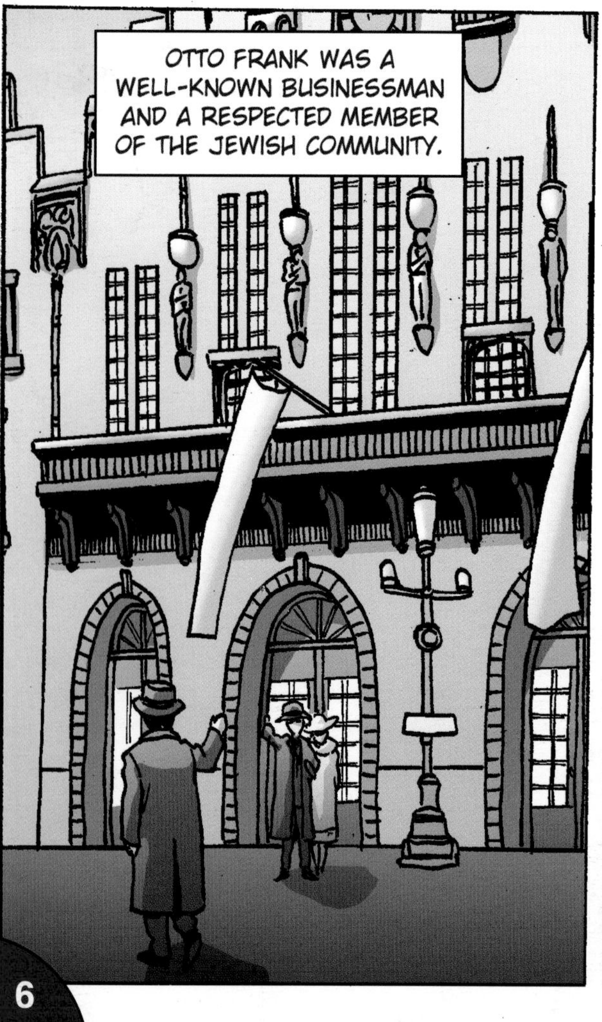
OTTO FRANK WAS A WELL-KNOWN BUSINESSMAN AND A RESPECTED MEMBER OF THE JEWISH COMMUNITY.

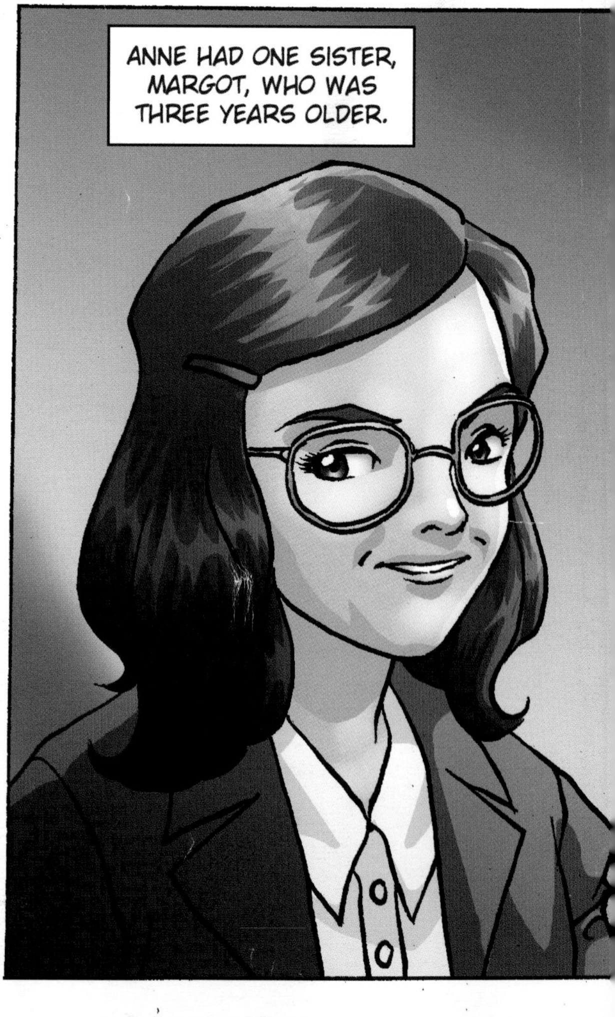
ANNE HAD ONE SISTER, MARGOT, WHO WAS THREE YEARS OLDER.

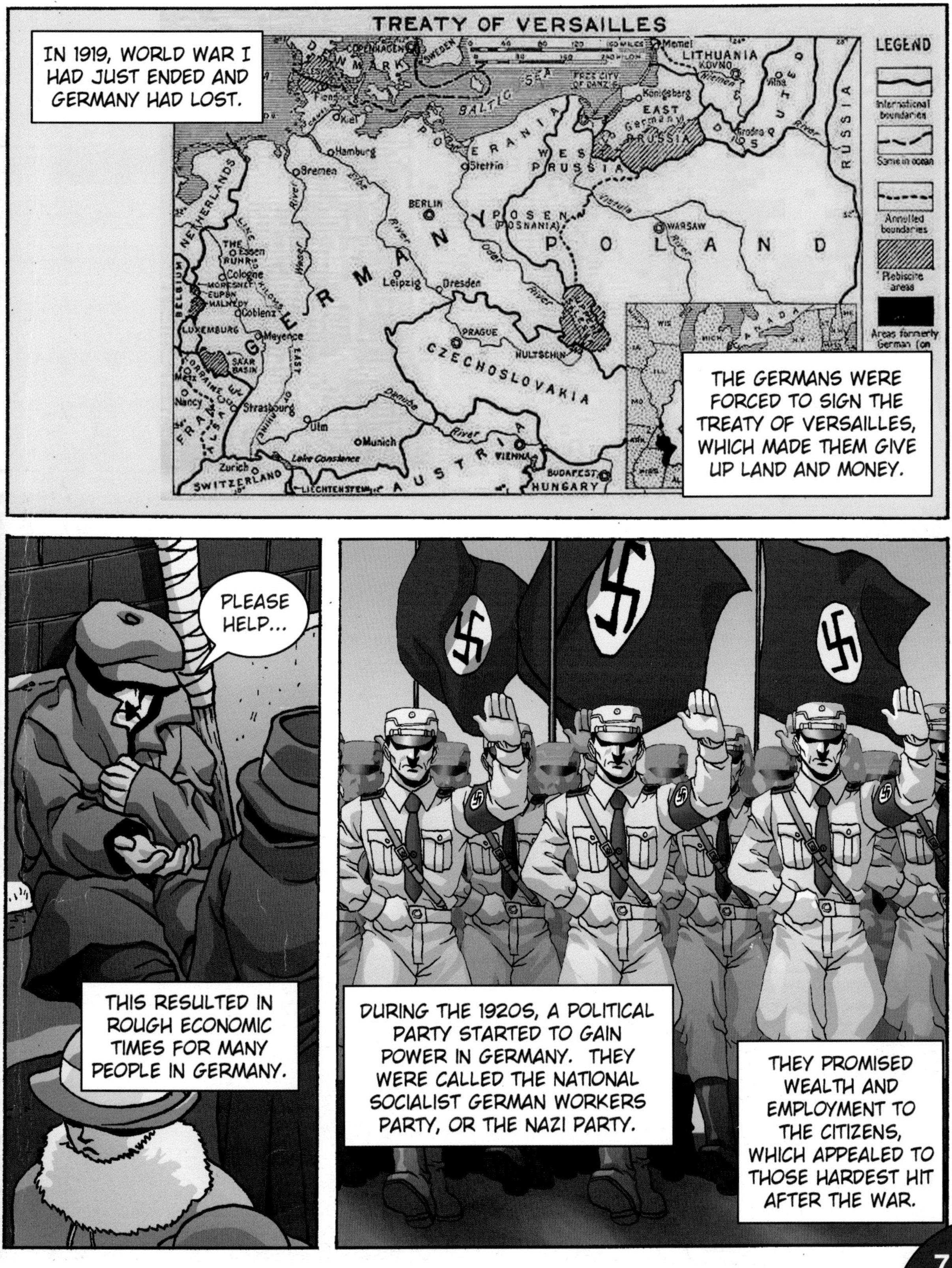

IN 1919, WORLD WAR I HAD JUST ENDED AND GERMANY HAD LOST.
TREATY OF VERSAILLES
LEGEND
International boundaries
Same in ocean
Annulled boundaries
Plebiscite areas
Areas formerly German (on
LITHUANIA
KOVNO
Memel
BALTIC SEA
FREE CITY OF DANZIG
Konigsberg
EAST PRUSSIA
RUSSIA
Kiel
Hamburg
Bremen
Stettin
POMERANIA
WEST PRUSSIA
NETHERLANDS
BERLIN
POSEN (POSNANIA)
WARSAW
POLAND
GERMANY
THE RUHR
Essen
Cologne
Leipzig
Dresden
BELGIUM
Coblenz
LUXEMBURG
Mayence
SAAR BASIN
PRAGUE
HULTSCHIN
CZECHOSLOVAKIA
Metz
Nancy
Strasbourg
Ulm
Munich
Lake Constance
VIENNA
BUDAPEST
HUNGARY
AUSTRIA
Zurich
SWITZERLAND
LIECHTENSTEIN
THE GERMANS WERE FORCED TO SIGN THE TREATY OF VERSAILLES, WHICH MADE THEM GIVE UP LAND AND MONEY.
PLEASE HELP...
THIS RESULTED IN ROUGH ECONOMIC TIMES FOR MANY PEOPLE IN GERMANY.
DURING THE 1920S, A POLITICAL PARTY STARTED TO GAIN POWER IN GERMANY. THEY WERE CALLED THE NATIONAL SOCIALIST GERMAN WORKERS PARTY, OR THE NAZI PARTY.
THEY PROMISED WEALTH AND EMPLOYMENT TO THE CITIZENS, WHICH APPEALED TO THOSE HARDEST HIT AFTER THE WAR.

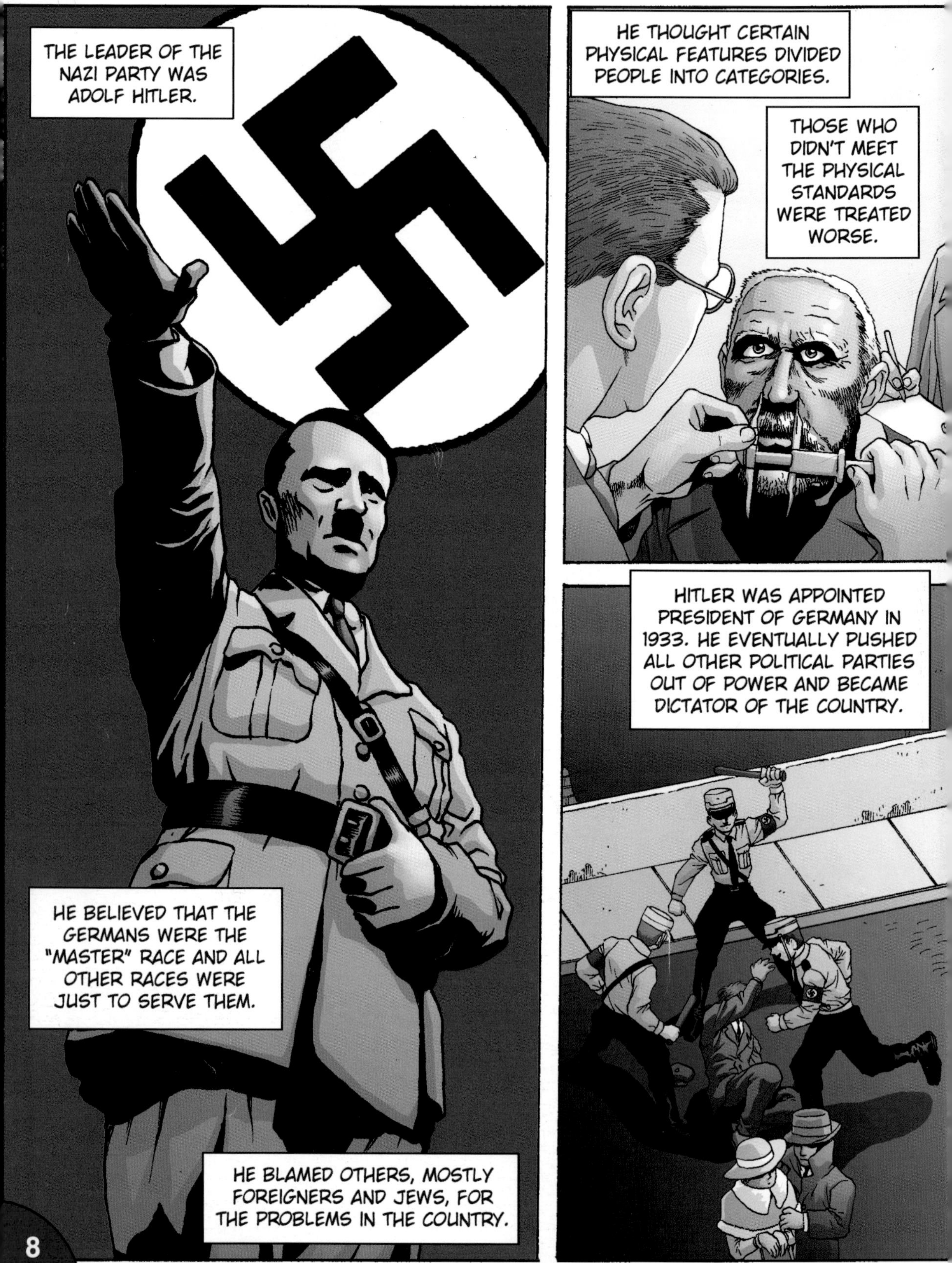
THE LEADER OF THE NAZI PARTY WAS ADOLF HITLER.
HE BELIEVED THAT THE GERMANS WERE THE "MASTER" RACE AND ALL OTHER RACES WERE JUST TO SERVE THEM.
HE BLAMED OTHERS, MOSTLY FOREIGNERS AND JEWS, FOR THE PROBLEMS IN THE COUNTRY.
HE THOUGHT CERTAIN PHYSICAL FEATURES DIVIDED PEOPLE INTO CATEGORIES.
THOSE WHO DIDN'T MEET THE PHYSICAL STANDARDS WERE TREATED WORSE.
HITLER WAS APPOINTED PRESIDENT OF GERMANY IN 1933. HE EVENTUALLY PUSHED ALL OTHER POLITICAL PARTIES OUT OF POWER AND BECAME DICTATOR OF THE COUNTRY.

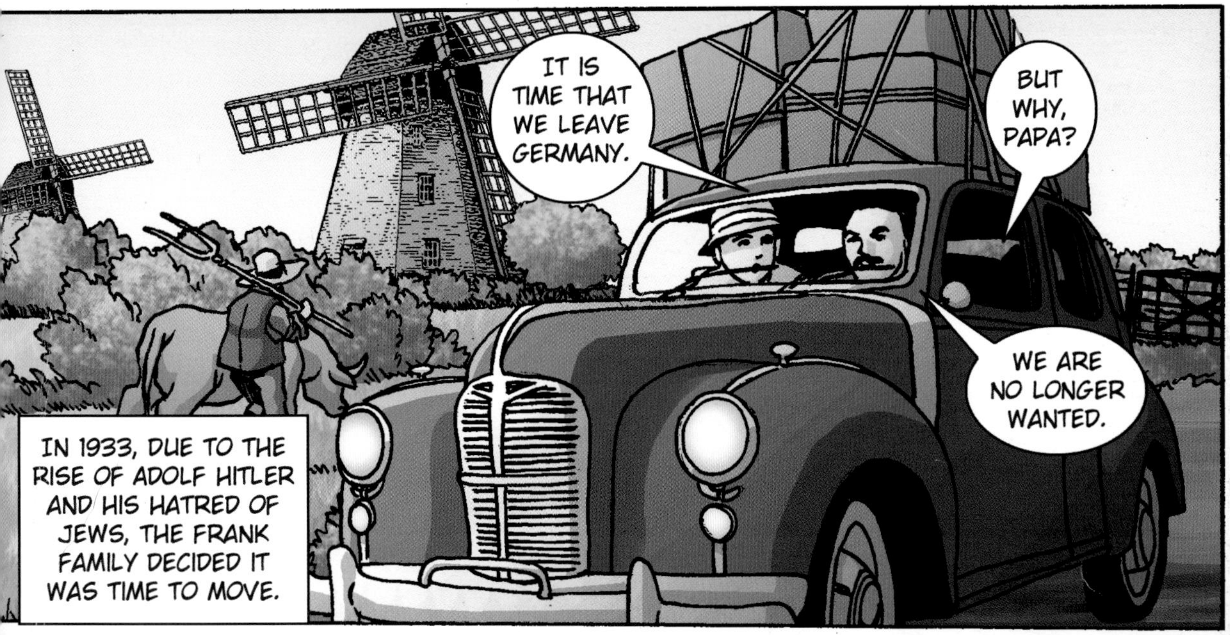
IN 1933, DUE TO THE RISE OF ADOLF HITLER AND HIS HATRED OF JEWS, THE FRANK FAMILY DECIDED IT WAS TIME TO MOVE.
IT IS TIME THAT WE LEAVE GERMANY.
BUT WHY, PAPA?
WE ARE NO LONGER WANTED.

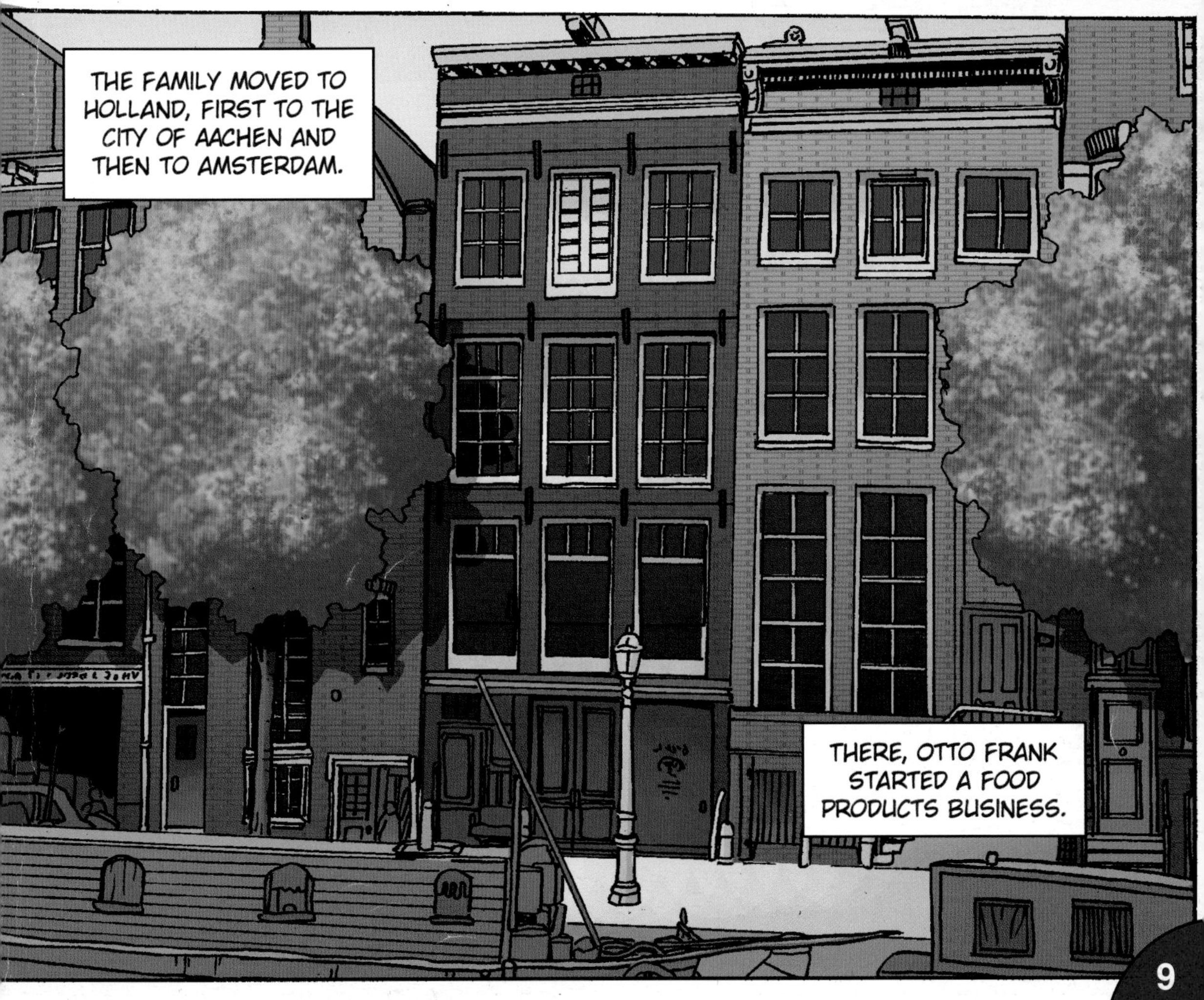
THE FAMILY MOVED TO HOLLAND, FIRST TO THE CITY OF AACHEN AND THEN TO AMSTERDAM.
THERE, OTTO FRANK STARTED A FOOD PRODUCTS BUSINESS.

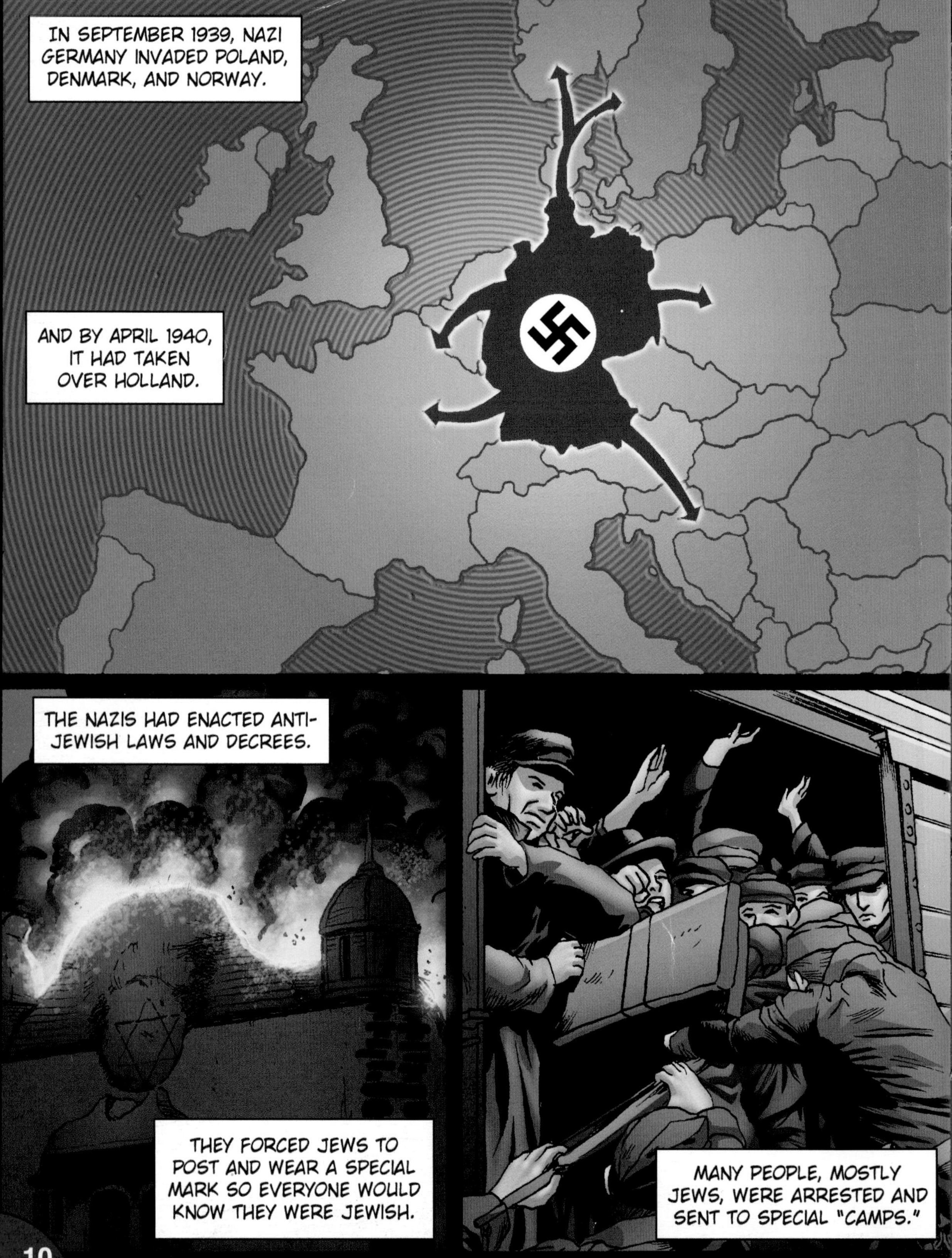
IN SEPTEMBER 1939, NAZI GERMANY INVADED POLAND, DENMARK, AND NORWAY.
AND BY APRIL 1940, IT HAD TAKEN OVER HOLLAND.
THE NAZIS HAD ENACTED ANTI-JEWISH LAWS AND DECREES.
THEY FORCED JEWS TO POST AND WEAR A SPECIAL MARK SO EVERYONE WOULD KNOW THEY WERE JEWISH.
MANY PEOPLE, MOSTLY JEWS, WERE ARRESTED AND SENT TO SPECIAL "CAMPS."

# Chapter 2 Anne's Diary

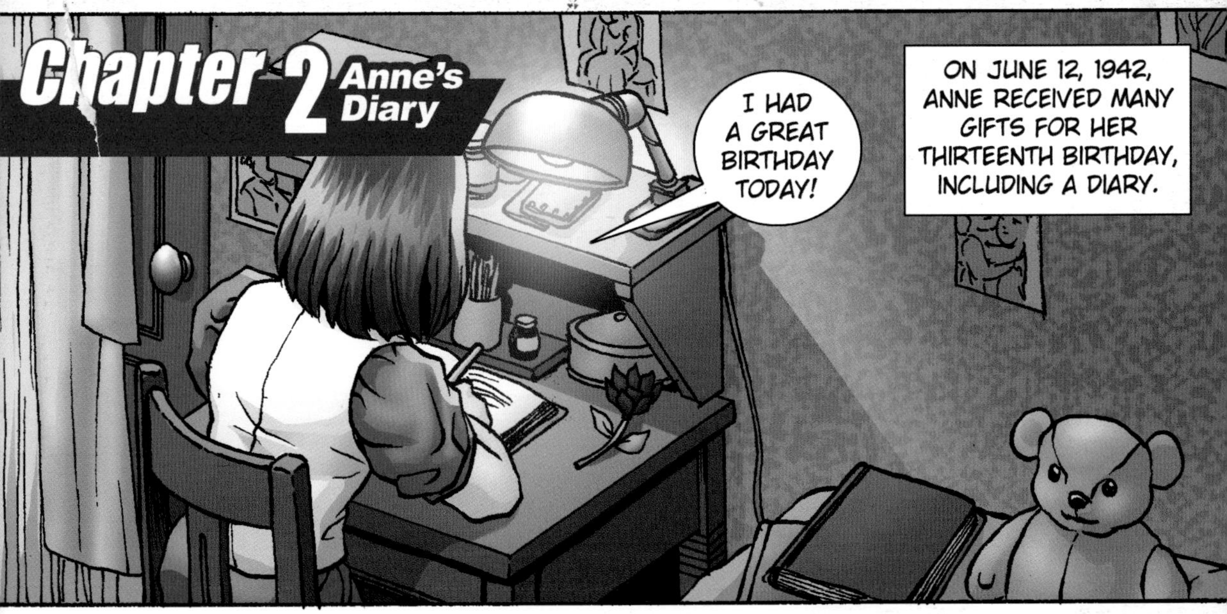
ON JUNE 12, 1942, ANNE RECEIVED MANY GIFTS FOR HER THIRTEENTH BIRTHDAY, INCLUDING A DIARY.
I HAD A GREAT BIRTHDAY TODAY!

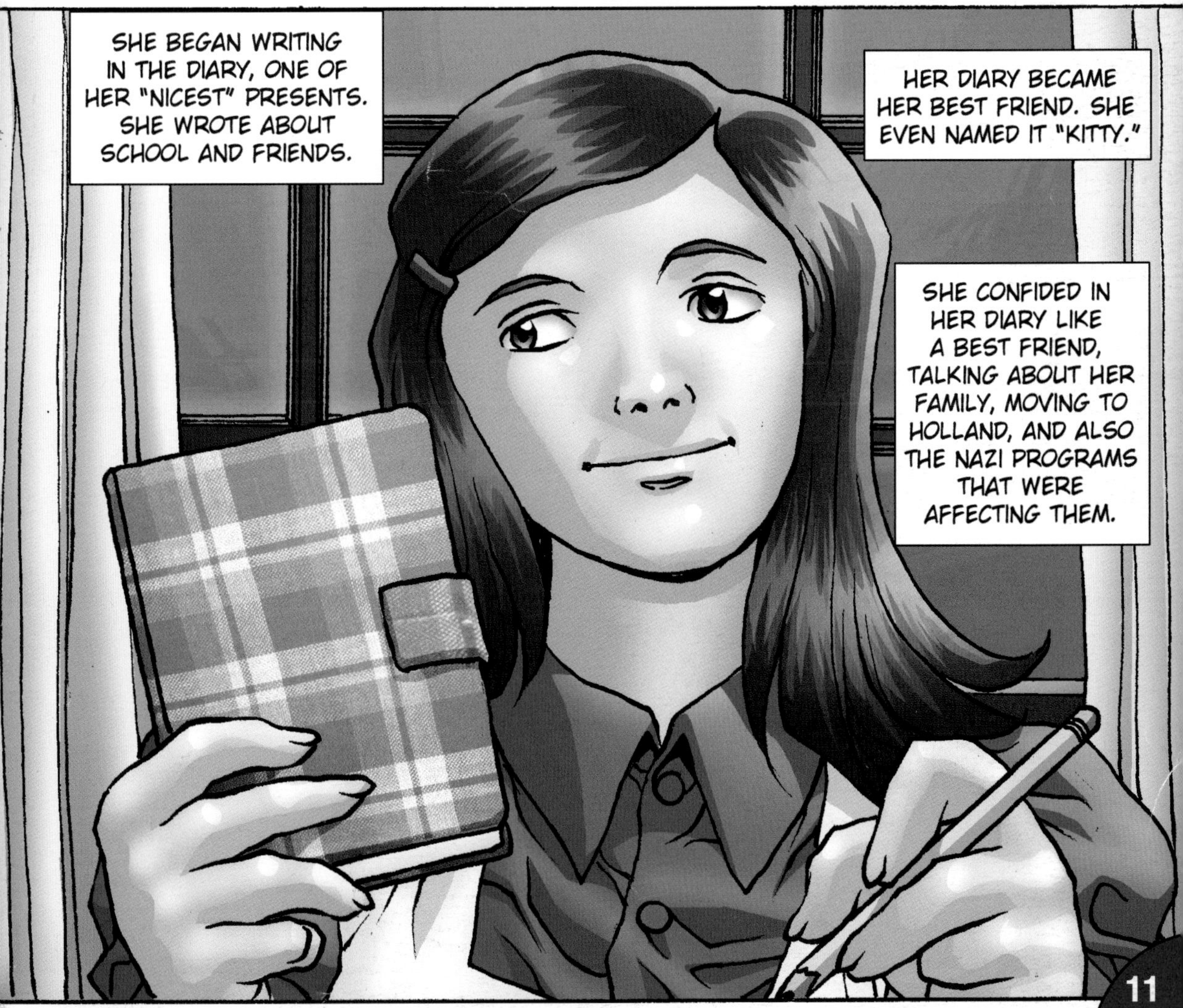
SHE BEGAN WRITING IN THE DIARY, ONE OF HER "NICEST" PRESENTS. SHE WROTE ABOUT SCHOOL AND FRIENDS.
HER DIARY BECAME HER BEST FRIEND. SHE EVEN NAMED IT "KITTY."
SHE CONFIDED IN HER DIARY LIKE A BEST FRIEND, TALKING ABOUT HER FAMILY, MOVING TO HOLLAND, AND ALSO THE NAZI PROGRAMS THAT WERE AFFECTING THEM.

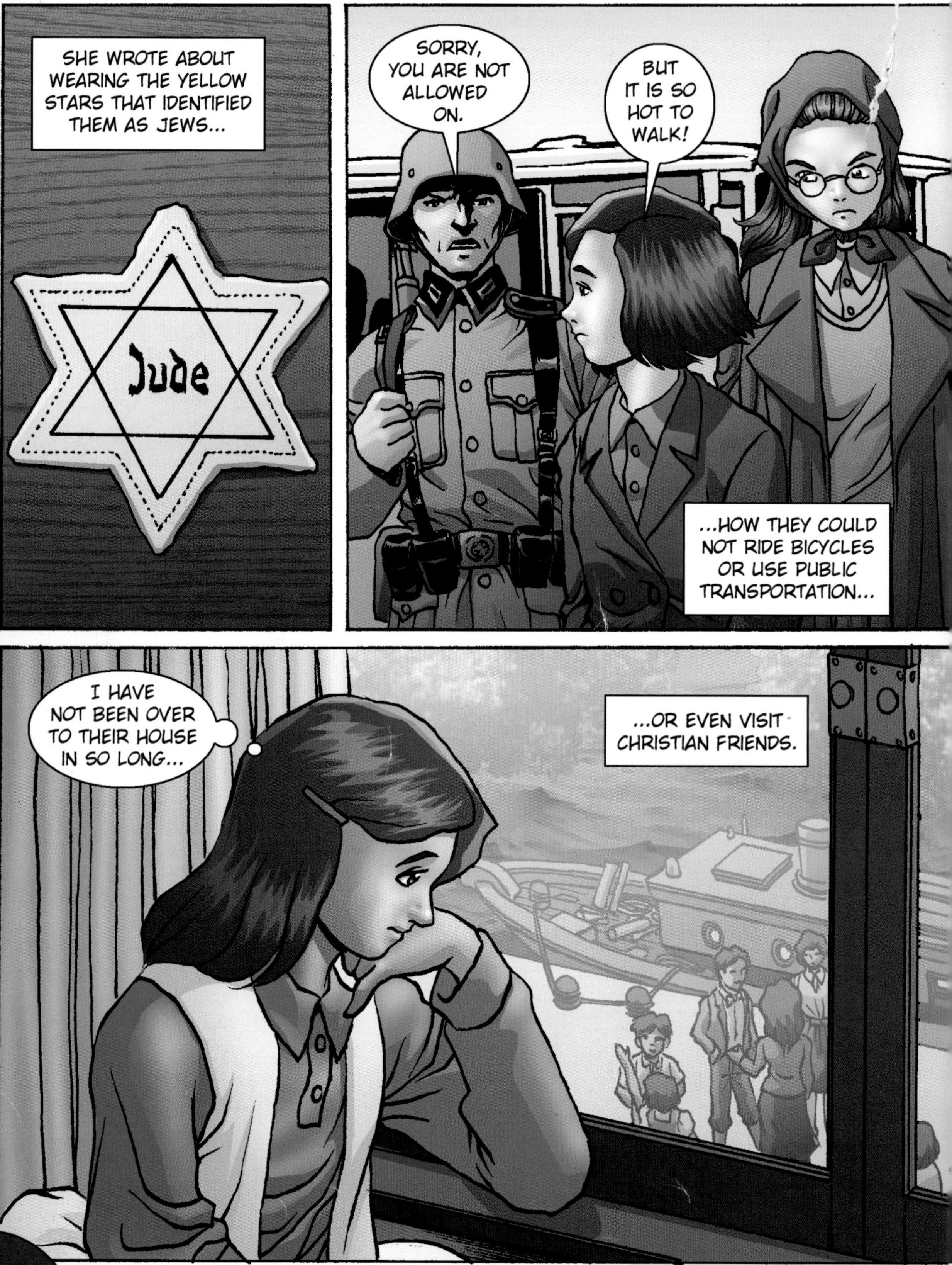
SHE WROTE ABOUT WEARING THE YELLOW STARS THAT IDENTIFIED THEM AS JEWS...
Jude
SORRY, YOU ARE NOT ALLOWED ON.
BUT IT IS SO HOT TO WALK!
...HOW THEY COULD NOT RIDE BICYCLES OR USE PUBLIC TRANSPORTATION...
I HAVE NOT BEEN OVER TO THEIR HOUSE IN SO LONG...
...OR EVEN VISIT CHRISTIAN FRIENDS.

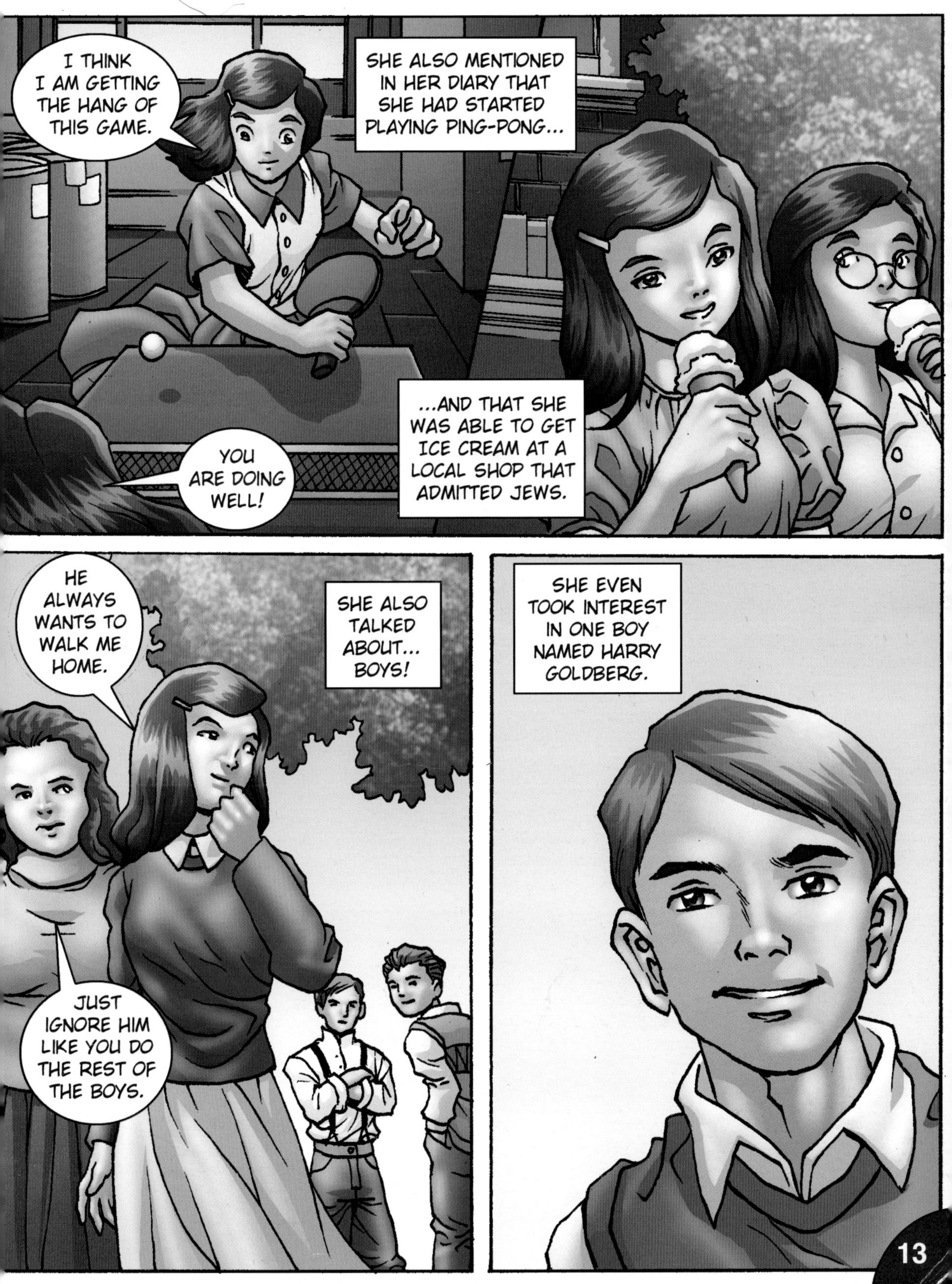
I THINK I AM GETTING THE HANG OF THIS GAME.
SHE ALSO MENTIONED IN HER DIARY THAT SHE HAD STARTED PLAYING PING-PONG...
YOU ARE DOING WELL!
...AND THAT SHE WAS ABLE TO GET ICE CREAM AT A LOCAL SHOP THAT ADMITTED JEWS.
HE ALWAYS WANTS TO WALK ME HOME.
SHE ALSO TALKED ABOUT... BOYS!
JUST IGNORE HIM LIKE YOU DO THE REST OF THE BOYS.
SHE EVEN TOOK INTEREST IN ONE BOY NAMED HARRY GOLDBERG.

# Chapter 3 The Secret Annex

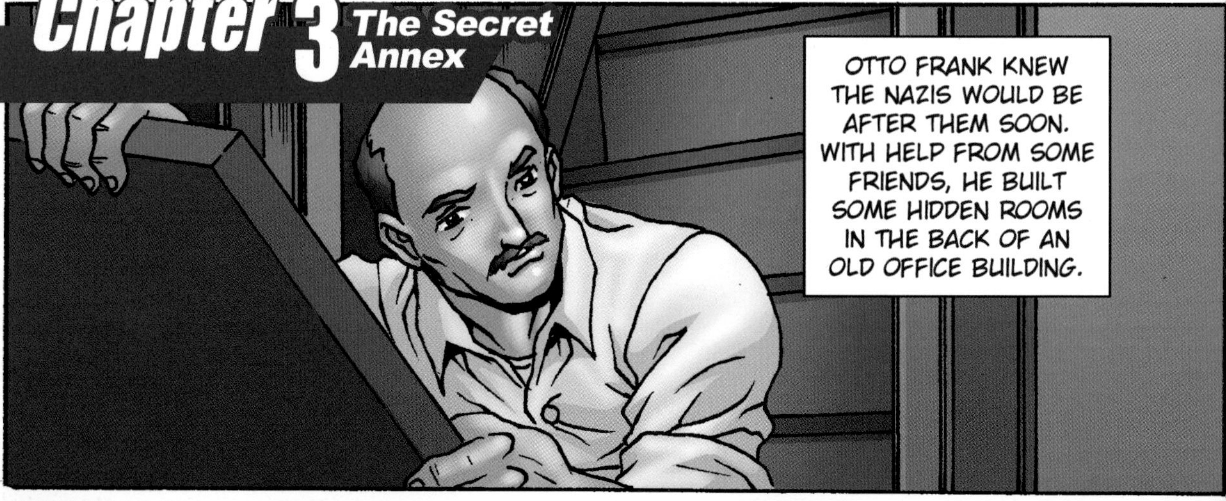
OTTO FRANK KNEW THE NAZIS WOULD BE AFTER THEM SOON. WITH HELP FROM SOME FRIENDS, HE BUILT SOME HIDDEN ROOMS IN THE BACK OF AN OLD OFFICE BUILDING.

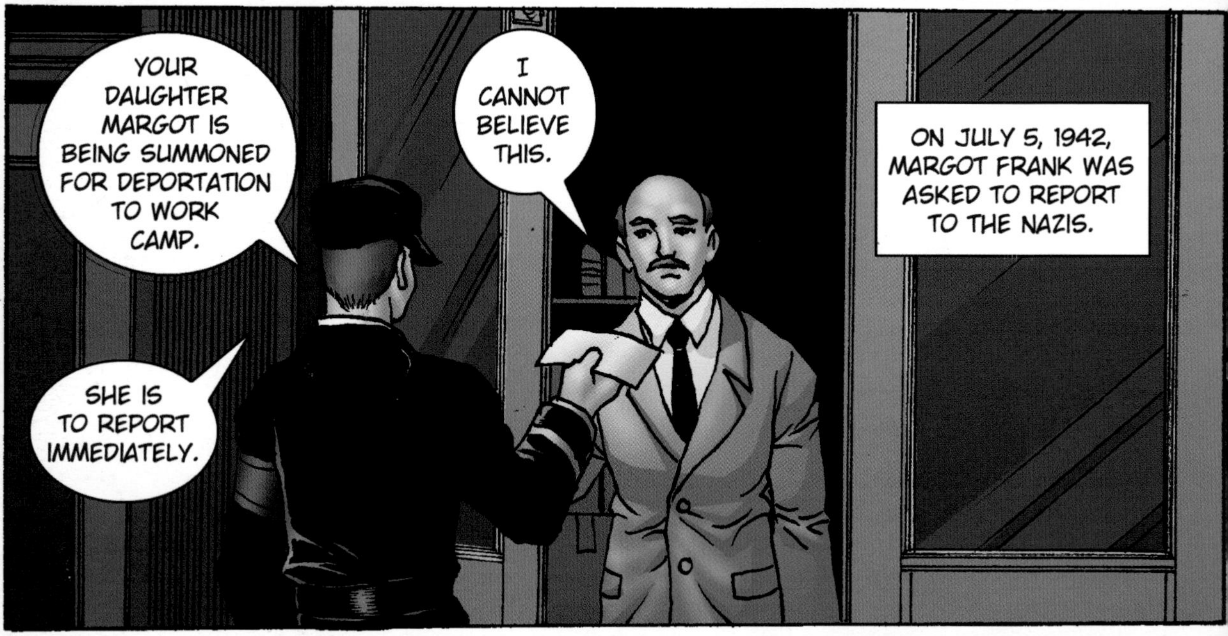
YOUR DAUGHTER MARGOT IS BEING SUMMONED FOR DEPORTATION TO WORK CAMP.
I CANNOT BELIEVE THIS.
ON JULY 5, 1942, MARGOT FRANK WAS ASKED TO REPORT TO THE NAZIS.
SHE IS TO REPORT IMMEDIATELY.

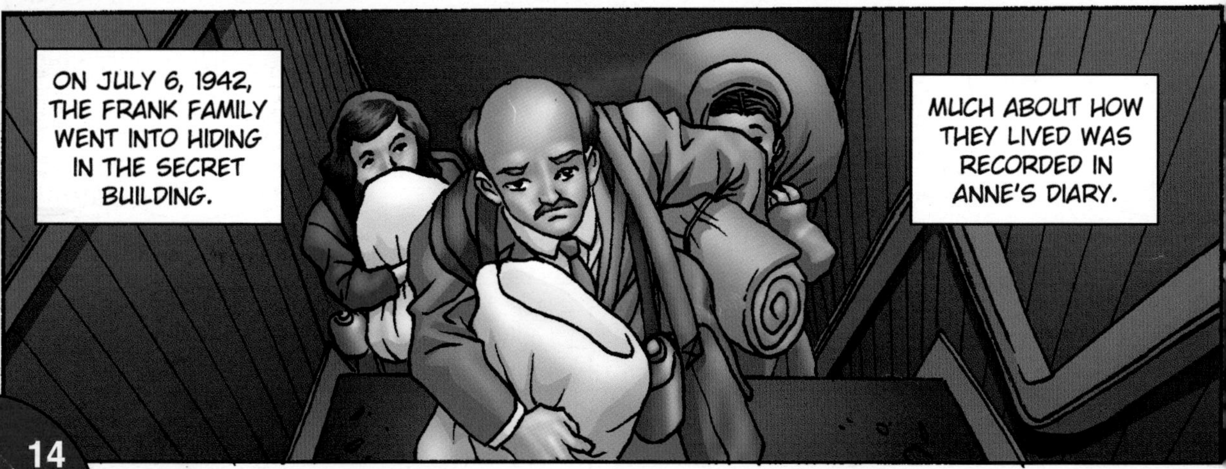
ON JULY 6, 1942, THE FRANK FAMILY WENT INTO HIDING IN THE SECRET BUILDING.
MUCH ABOUT HOW THEY LIVED WAS RECORDED IN ANNE'S DIARY.

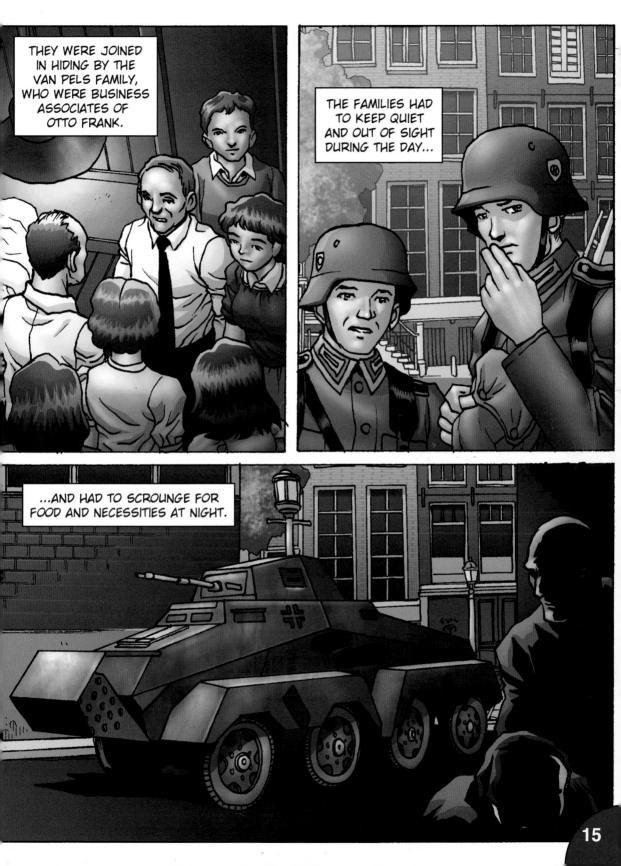

THEY WERE JOINED IN HIDING BY THE VAN PELS FAMILY, WHO WERE BUSINESS ASSOCIATES OF OTTO FRANK.

THE FAMILIES HAD TO KEEP QUIET AND OUT OF SIGHT DURING THE DAY...

...AND HAD TO SCROUNGE FOR FOOD AND NECESSITIES AT NIGHT.

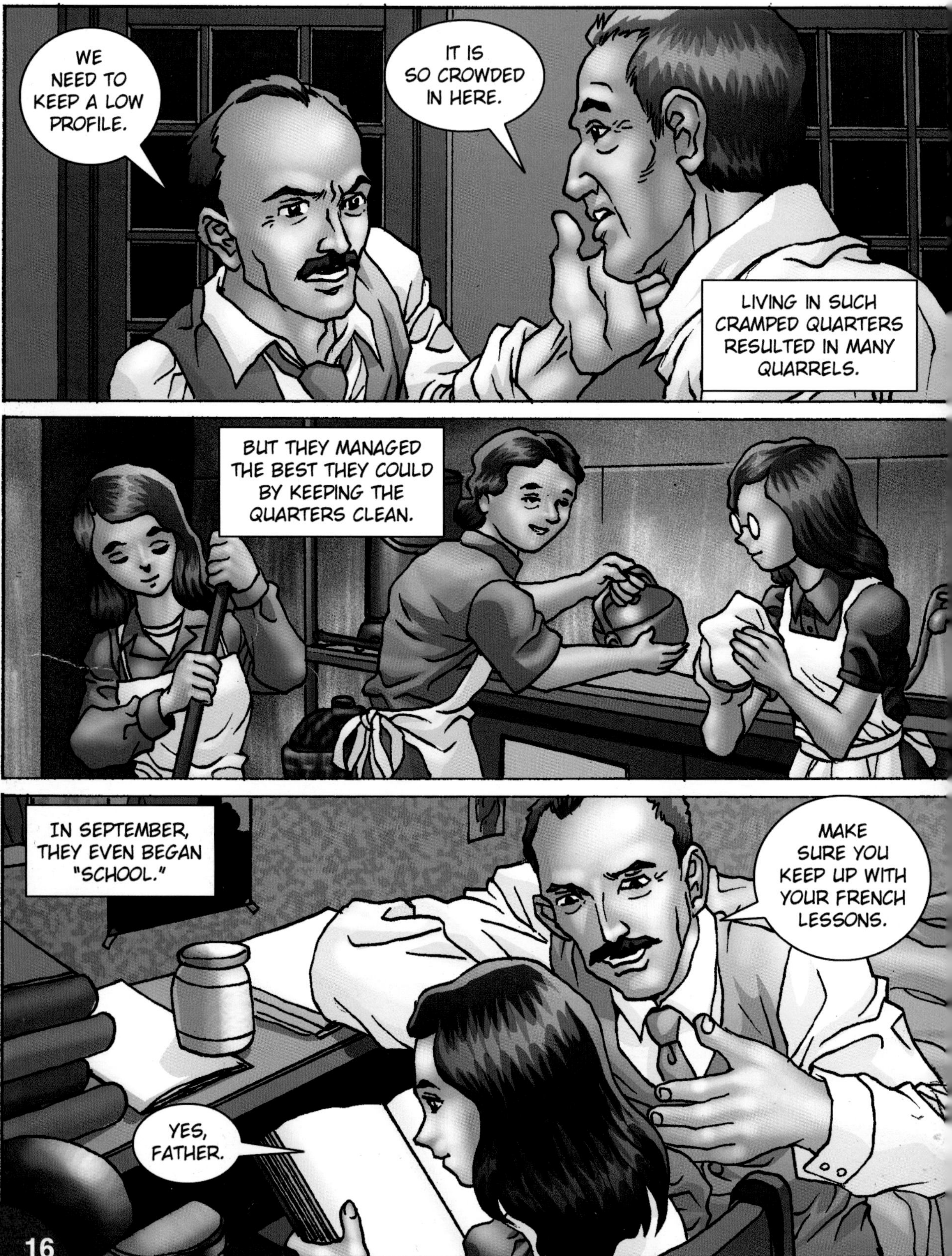
WE NEED TO KEEP A LOW PROFILE.
IT IS SO CROWDED IN HERE.
LIVING IN SUCH CRAMPED QUARTERS RESULTED IN MANY QUARRELS.
BUT THEY MANAGED THE BEST THEY COULD BY KEEPING THE QUARTERS CLEAN.
IN SEPTEMBER, THEY EVEN BEGAN "SCHOOL."
MAKE SURE YOU KEEP UP WITH YOUR FRENCH LESSONS.
YES, FATHER.

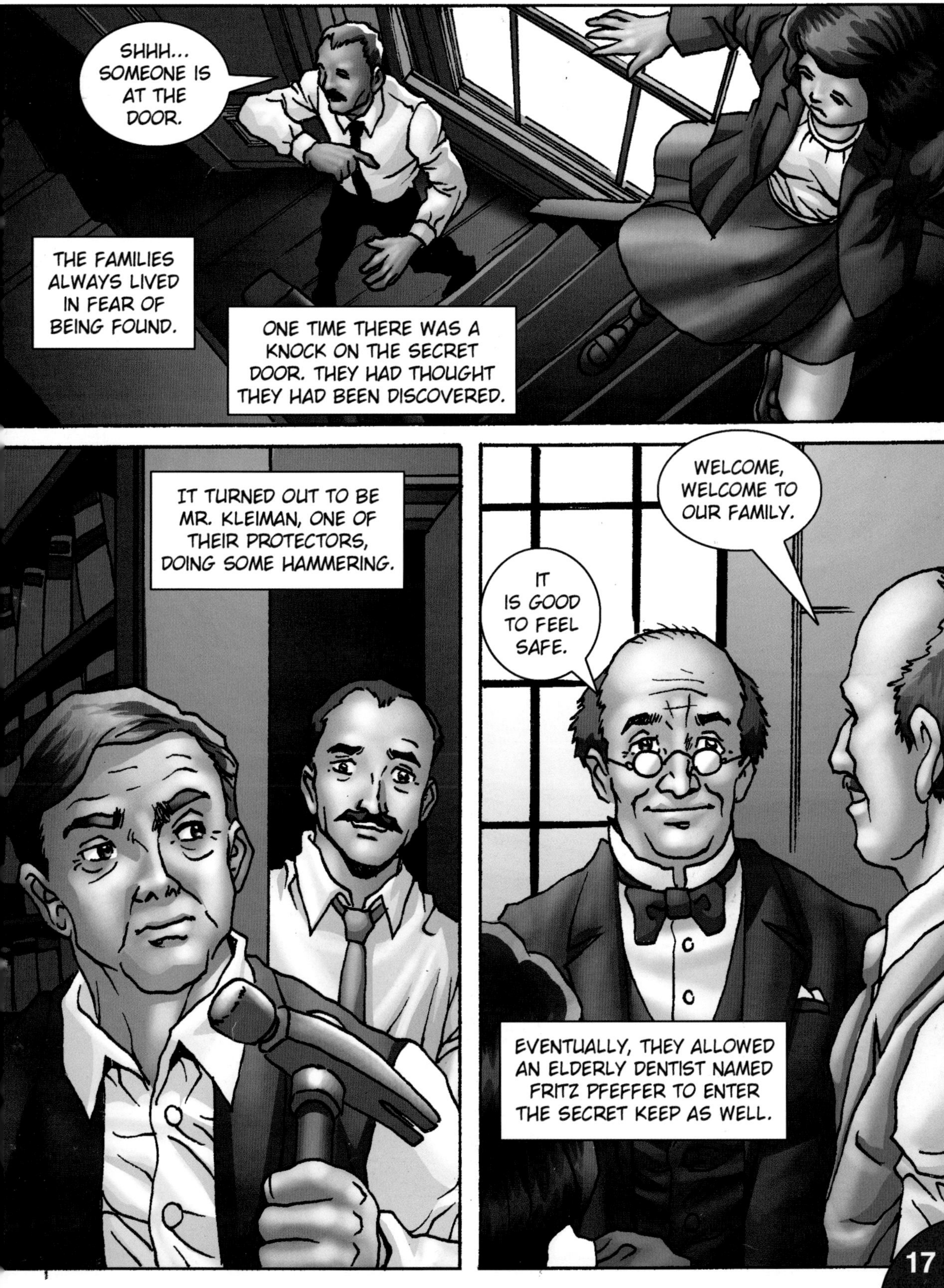
SHHH... SOMEONE IS AT THE DOOR.
THE FAMILIES ALWAYS LIVED IN FEAR OF BEING FOUND.
ONE TIME THERE WAS A KNOCK ON THE SECRET DOOR. THEY HAD THOUGHT THEY HAD BEEN DISCOVERED.
IT TURNED OUT TO BE MR. KLEIMAN, ONE OF THEIR PROTECTORS, DOING SOME HAMMERING.
WELCOME, WELCOME TO OUR FAMILY.
IT IS GOOD TO FEEL SAFE.
EVENTUALLY, THEY ALLOWED AN ELDERLY DENTIST NAMED FRITZ PFEFFER TO ENTER THE SECRET KEEP AS WELL.

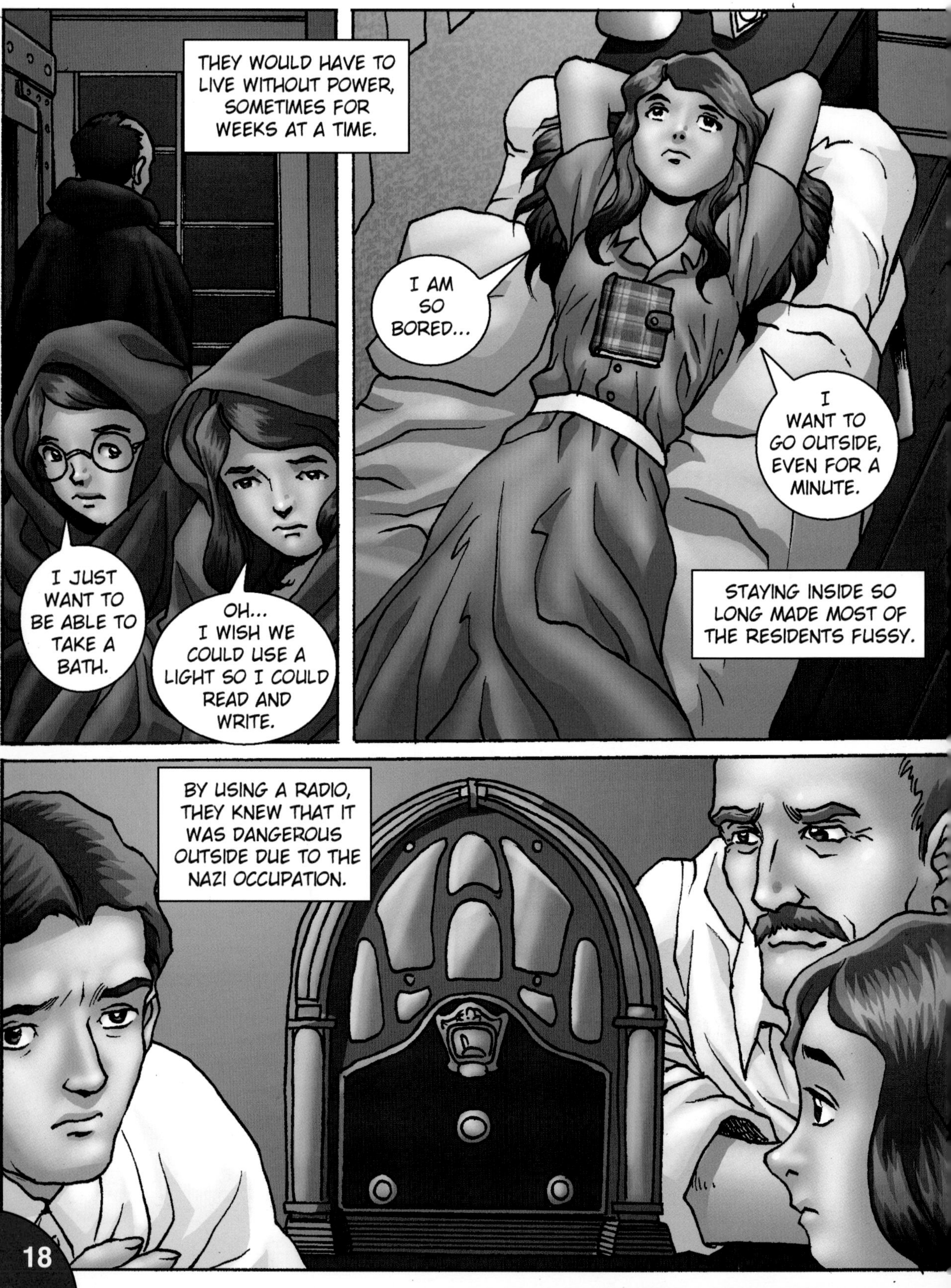
THEY WOULD HAVE TO LIVE WITHOUT POWER, SOMETIMES FOR WEEKS AT A TIME.
I JUST WANT TO BE ABLE TO TAKE A BATH.
OH... I WISH WE COULD USE A LIGHT SO I COULD READ AND WRITE.
I AM SO BORED...
I WANT TO GO OUTSIDE, EVEN FOR A MINUTE.
STAYING INSIDE SO LONG MADE MOST OF THE RESIDENTS FUSSY.
BY USING A RADIO, THEY KNEW THAT IT WAS DANGEROUS OUTSIDE DUE TO THE NAZI OCCUPATION.

# Chapter 4 Fear of Discovery

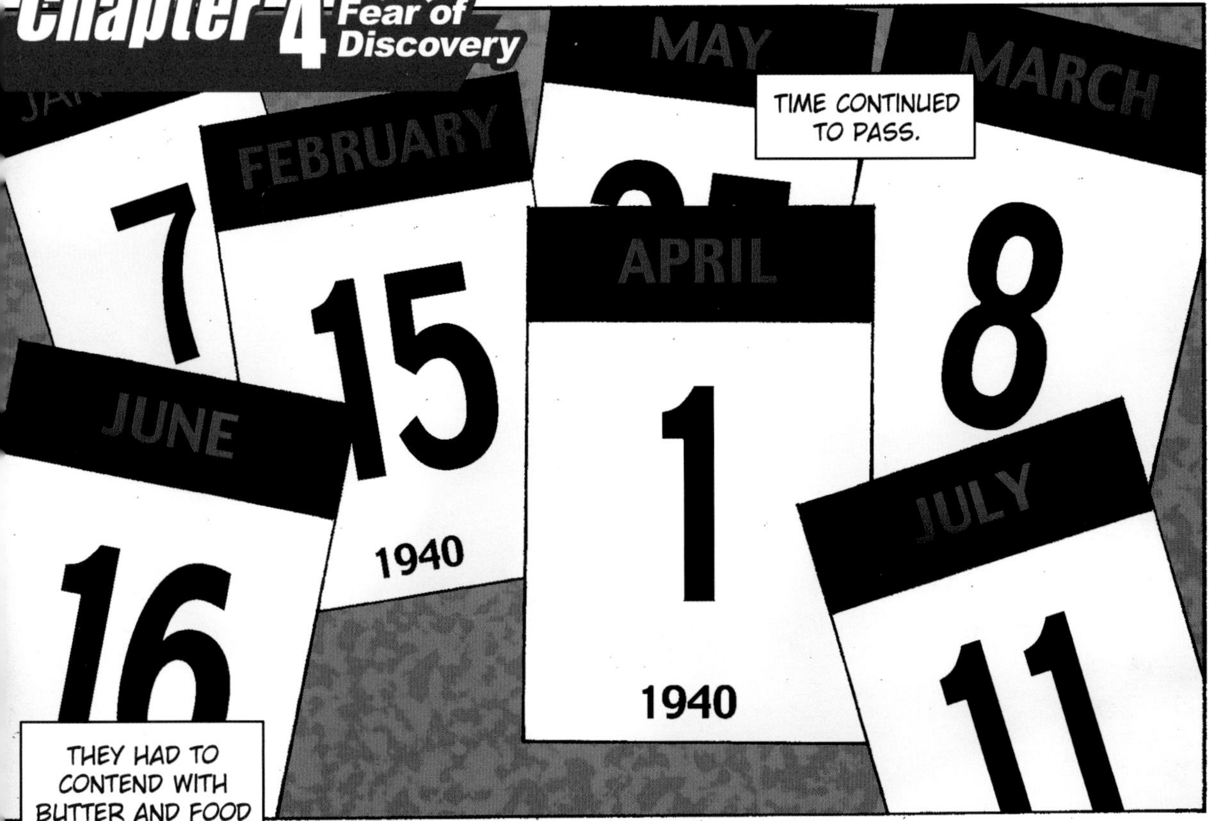
TIME CONTINUED TO PASS.
MAY
MARCH
FEBRUARY
7
15
1940
APRIL
1
1940
8
JUNE
16
JULY
11

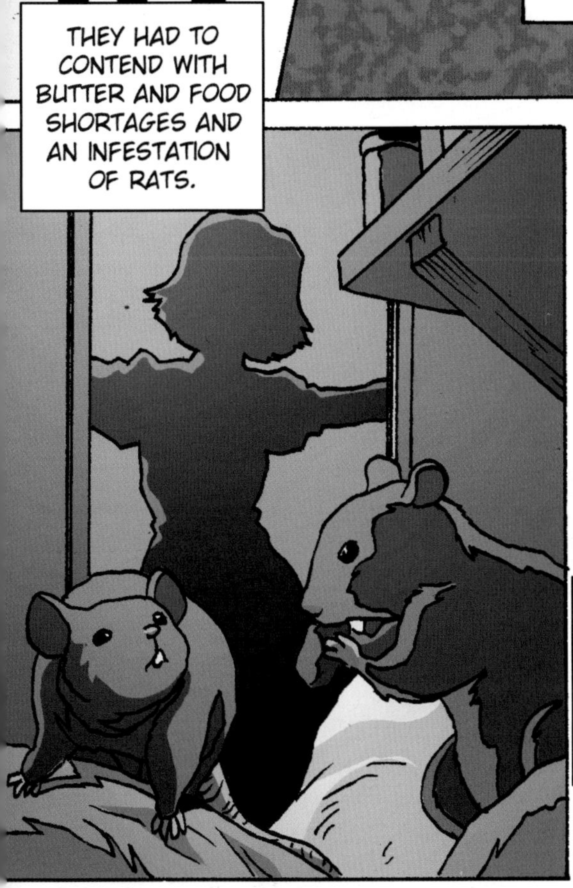
THEY HAD TO CONTEND WITH BUTTER AND FOOD SHORTAGES AND AN INFESTATION OF RATS.

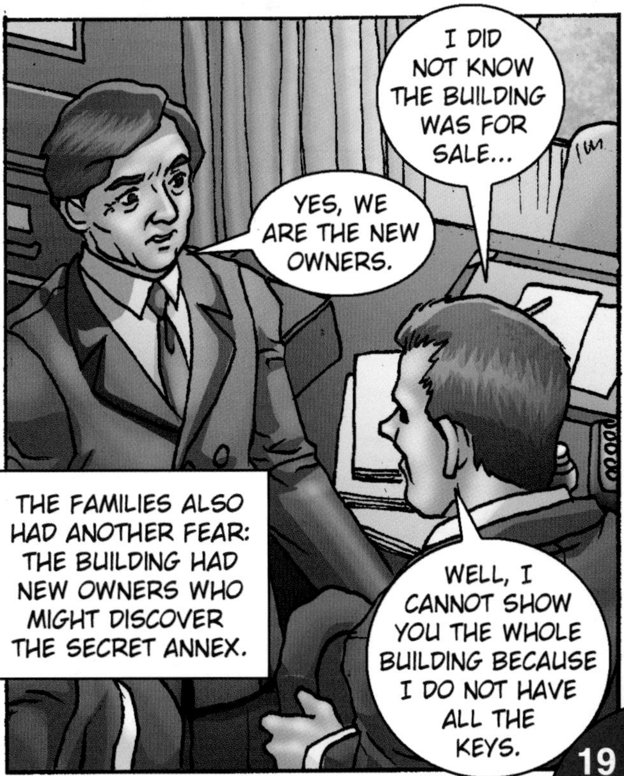
I DID NOT KNOW THE BUILDING WAS FOR SALE...
YES, WE ARE THE NEW OWNERS.
THE FAMILIES ALSO HAD ANOTHER FEAR: THE BUILDING HAD NEW OWNERS WHO MIGHT DISCOVER THE SECRET ANNEX.
WELL, I CANNOT SHOW YOU THE WHOLE BUILDING BECAUSE I DO NOT HAVE ALL THE KEYS.

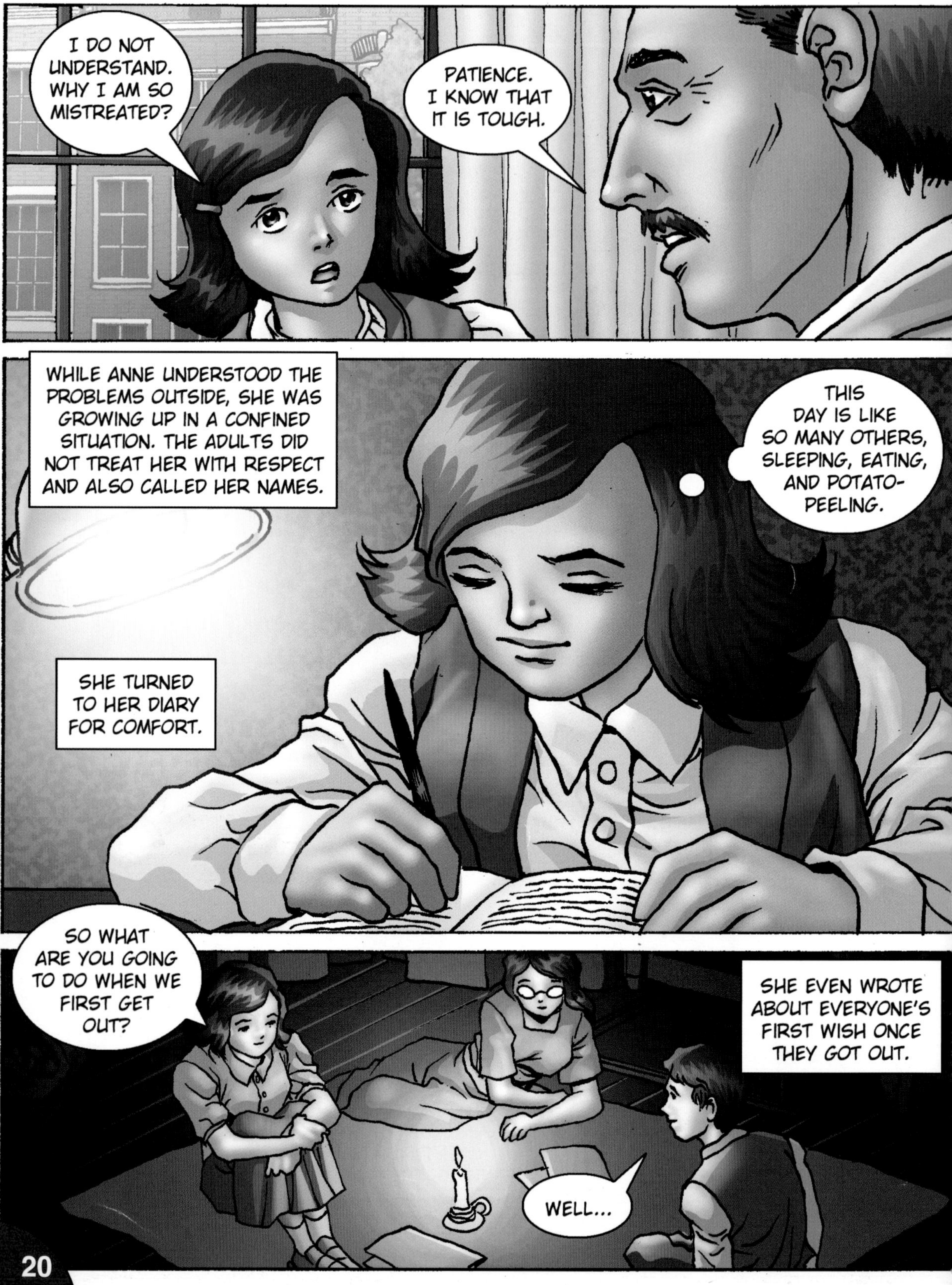
I DO NOT UNDERSTAND. WHY I AM SO MISTREATED?
PATIENCE. I KNOW THAT IT IS TOUGH.
WHILE ANNE UNDERSTOOD THE PROBLEMS OUTSIDE, SHE WAS GROWING UP IN A CONFINED SITUATION. THE ADULTS DID NOT TREAT HER WITH RESPECT AND ALSO CALLED HER NAMES.
THIS DAY IS LIKE SO MANY OTHERS, SLEEPING, EATING, AND POTATO-PEELING.
SHE TURNED TO HER DIARY FOR COMFORT.
SO WHAT ARE YOU GOING TO DO WHEN WE FIRST GET OUT?
SHE EVEN WROTE ABOUT EVERYONE'S FIRST WISH ONCE THEY GOT OUT.
WELL...

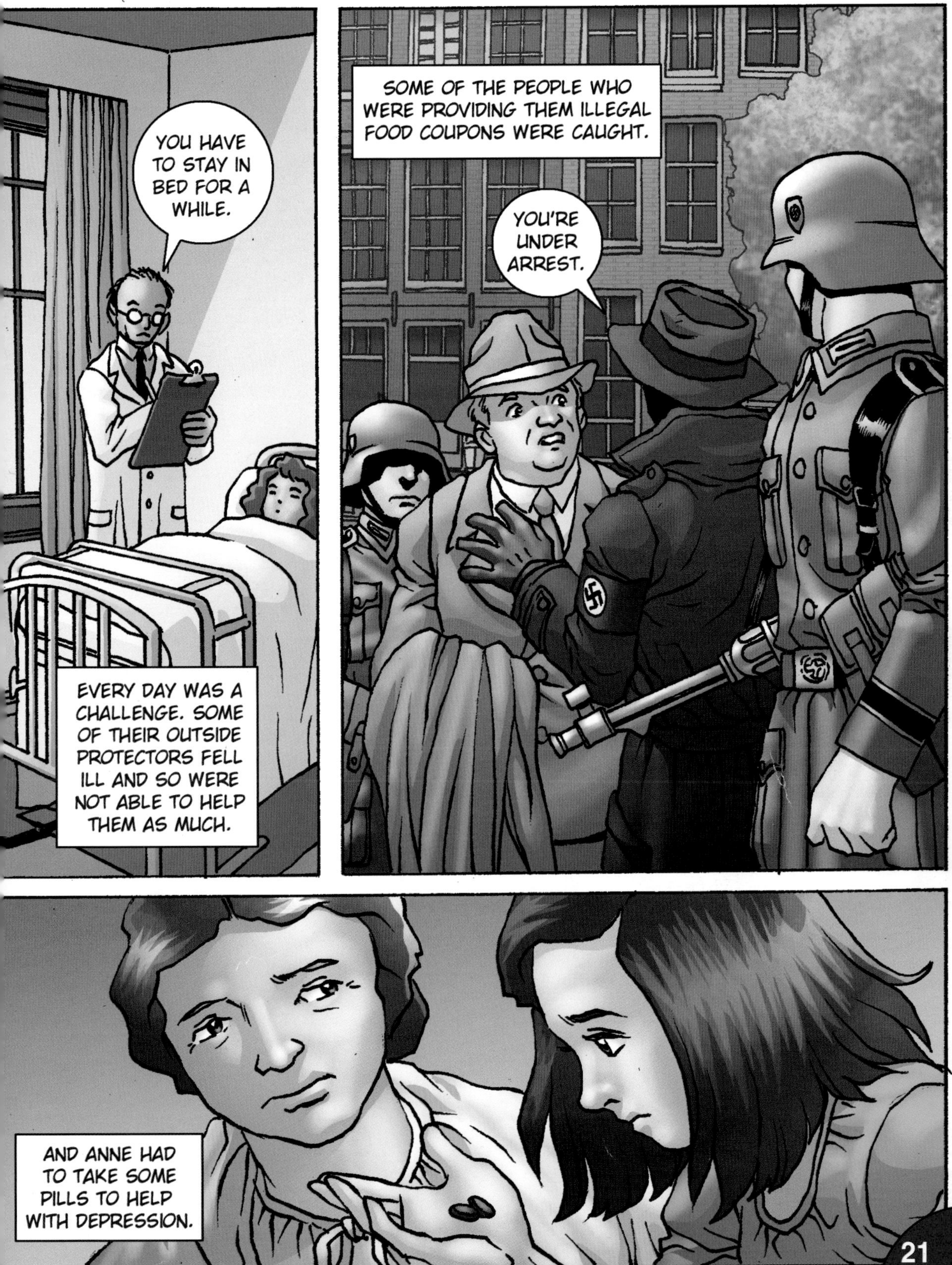
YOU HAVE TO STAY IN BED FOR A WHILE.
EVERY DAY WAS A CHALLENGE. SOME OF THEIR OUTSIDE PROTECTORS FELL ILL AND SO WERE NOT ABLE TO HELP THEM AS MUCH.
SOME OF THE PEOPLE WHO WERE PROVIDING THEM ILLEGAL FOOD COUPONS WERE CAUGHT.
YOU'RE UNDER ARREST.
AND ANNE HAD TO TAKE SOME PILLS TO HELP WITH DEPRESSION.

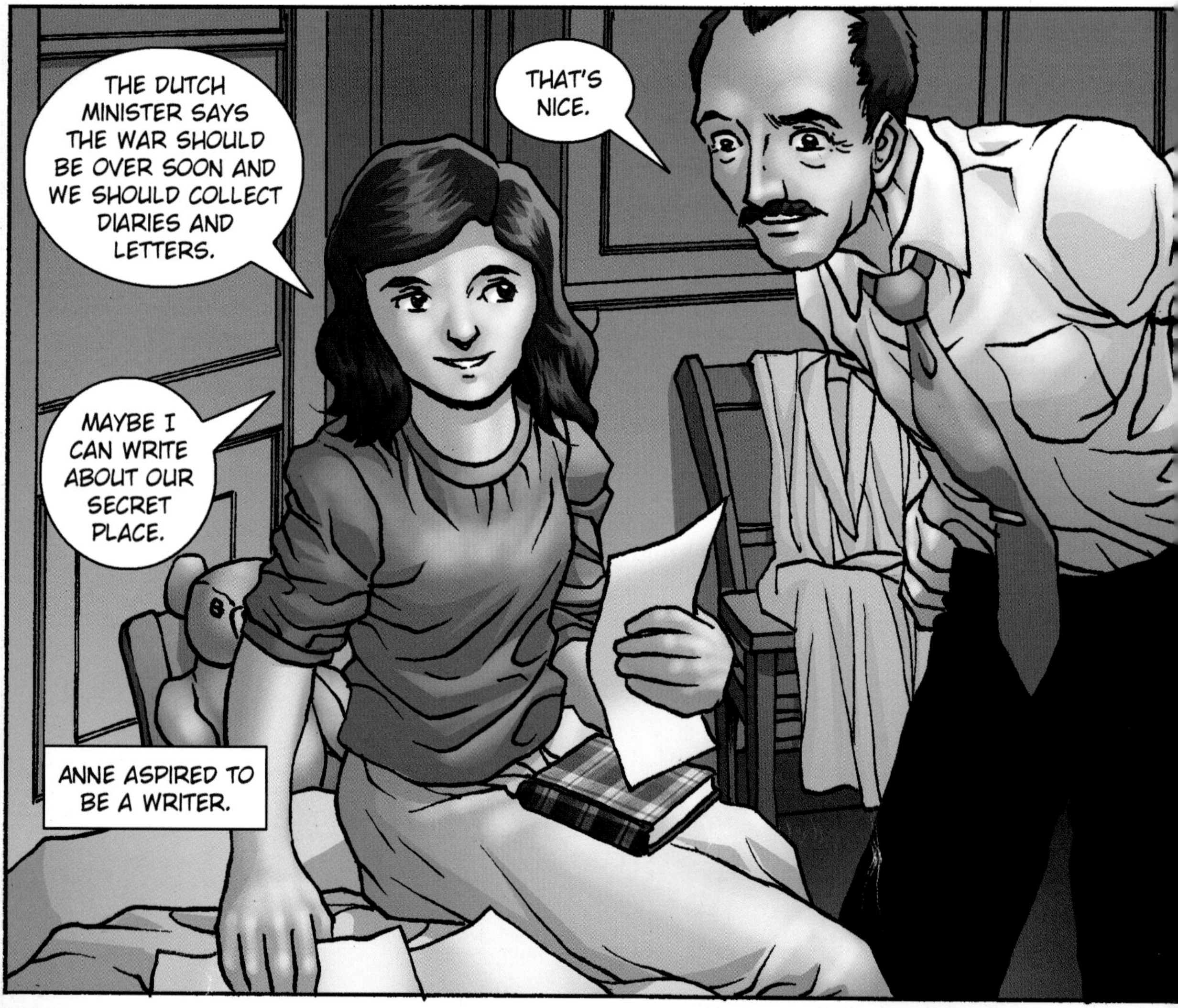
THE DUTCH MINISTER SAYS THE WAR SHOULD BE OVER SOON AND WE SHOULD COLLECT DIARIES AND LETTERS.
THAT'S NICE.
MAYBE I CAN WRITE ABOUT OUR SECRET PLACE.
ANNE ASPIRED TO BE A WRITER.

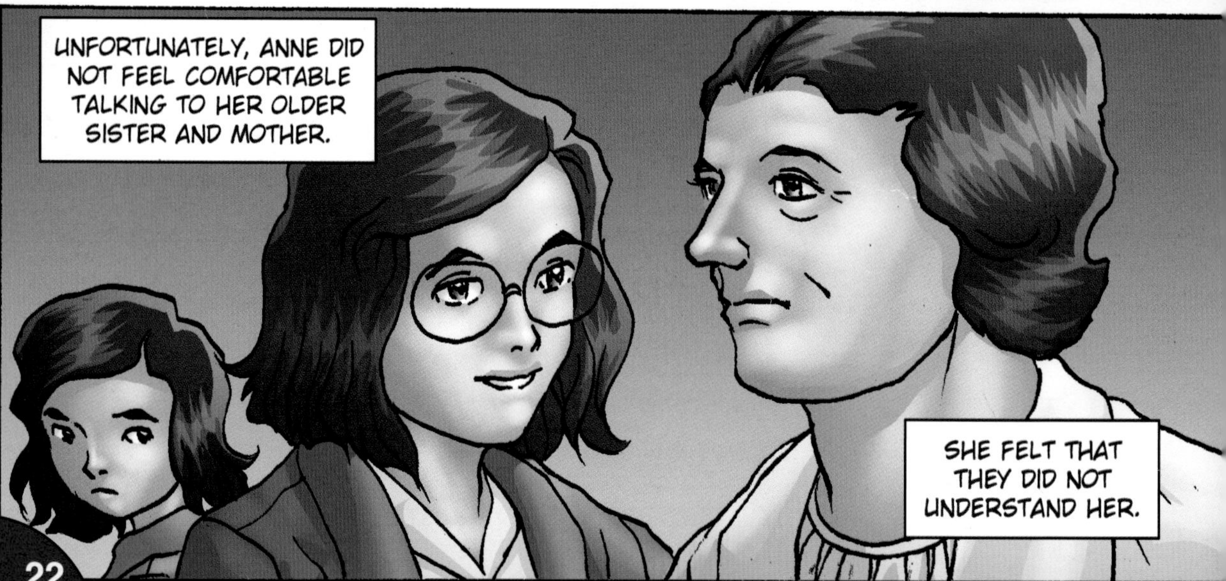
UNFORTUNATELY, ANNE DID NOT FEEL COMFORTABLE TALKING TO HER OLDER SISTER AND MOTHER.
SHE FELT THAT THEY DID NOT UNDERSTAND HER.

# Chapter 5 Days of Boredom

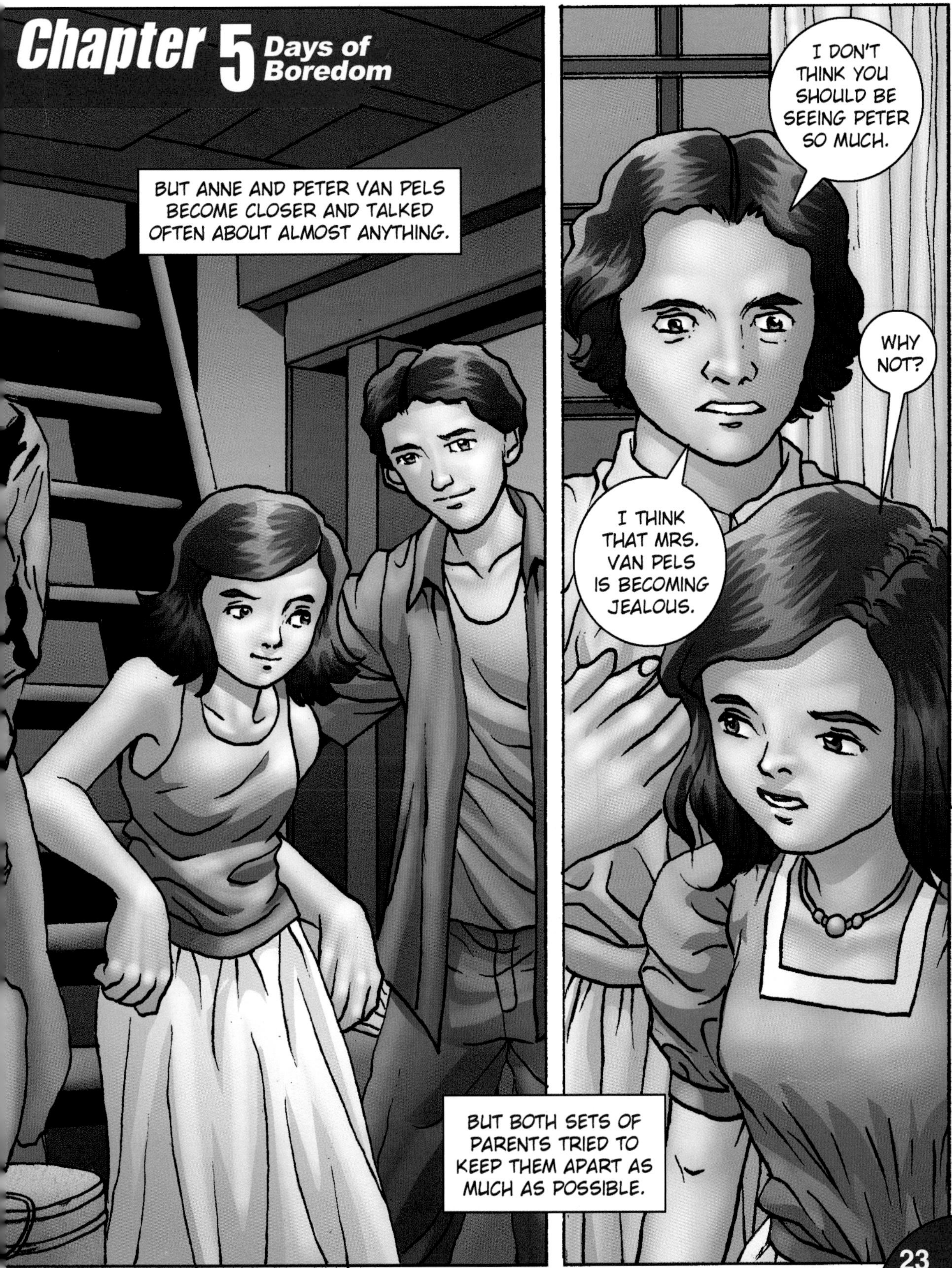
BUT ANNE AND PETER VAN PELS BECOME CLOSER AND TALKED OFTEN ABOUT ALMOST ANYTHING.
I DON'T THINK YOU SHOULD BE SEEING PETER SO MUCH.
WHY NOT?
I THINK THAT MRS. VAN PELS IS BECOMING JEALOUS.
BUT BOTH SETS OF PARENTS TRIED TO KEEP THEM APART AS MUCH AS POSSIBLE.

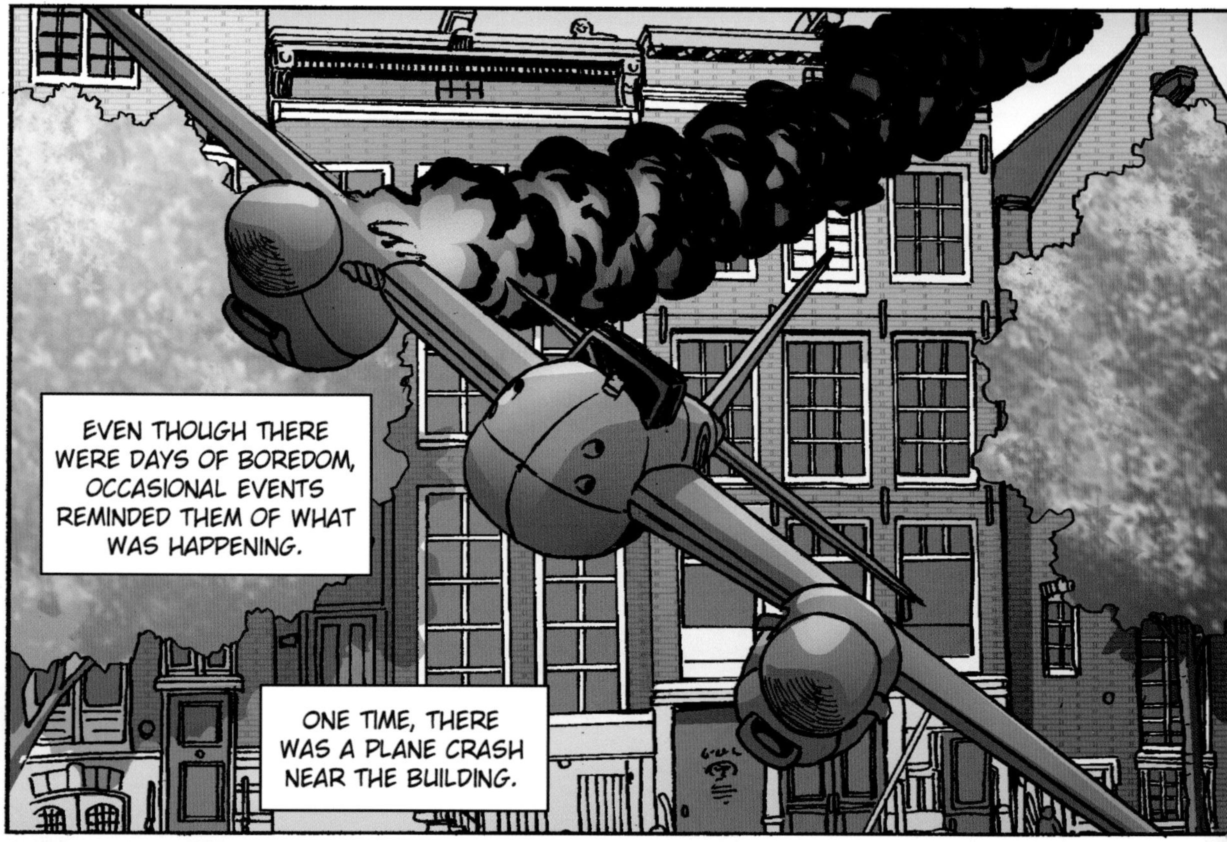
EVEN THOUGH THERE WERE DAYS OF BOREDOM, OCCASIONAL EVENTS REMINDED THEM OF WHAT WAS HAPPENING.
ONE TIME, THERE WAS A PLANE CRASH NEAR THE BUILDING.

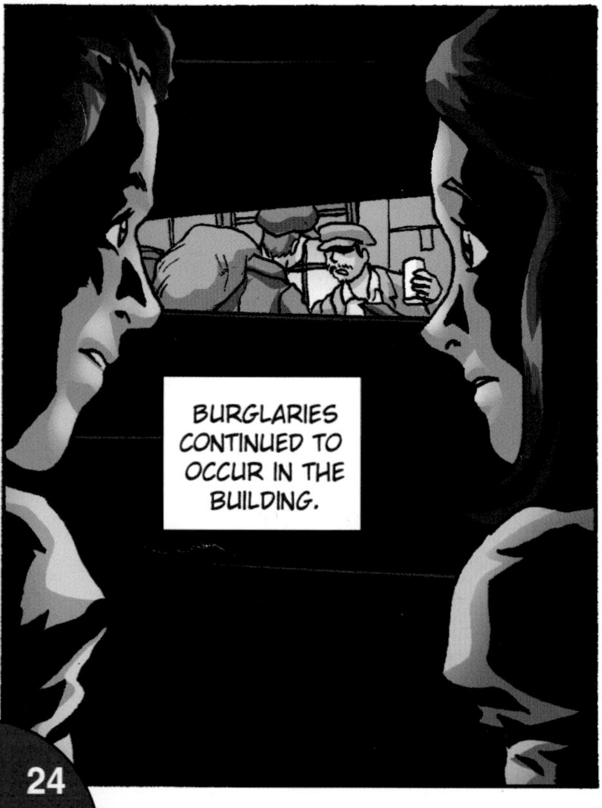
BURGLARIES CONTINUED TO OCCUR IN THE BUILDING.

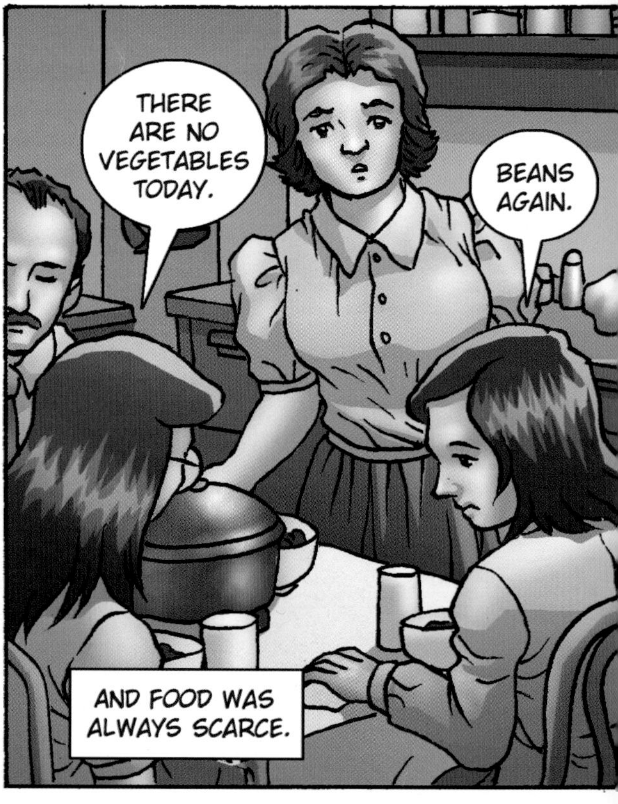
THERE ARE NO VEGETABLES TODAY.
BEANS AGAIN.
AND FOOD WAS ALWAYS SCARCE.

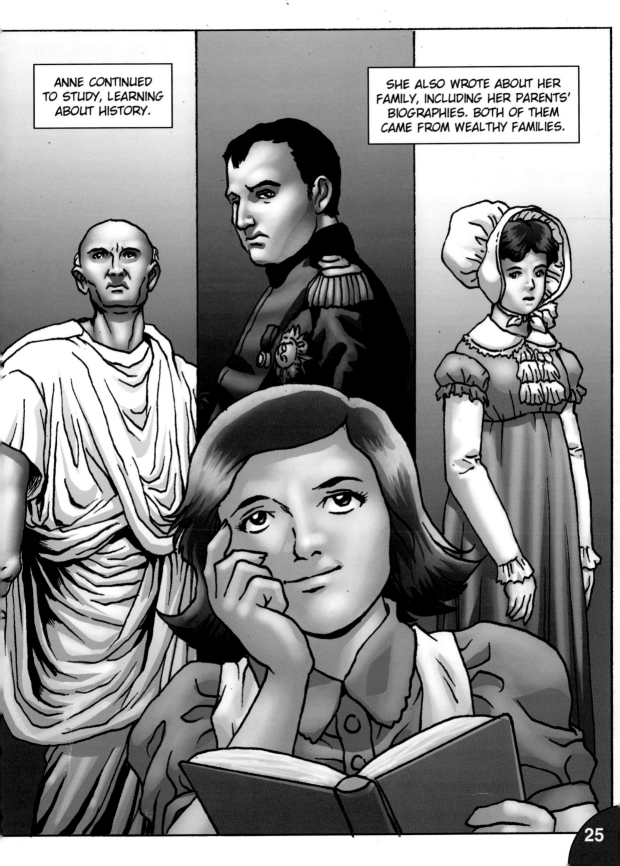

ANNE CONTINUED TO STUDY, LEARNING ABOUT HISTORY.

SHE ALSO WROTE ABOUT HER FAMILY, INCLUDING HER PARENTS' BIOGRAPHIES. BOTH OF THEM CAME FROM WEALTHY FAMILIES.

# Chapter 6 The War Ends

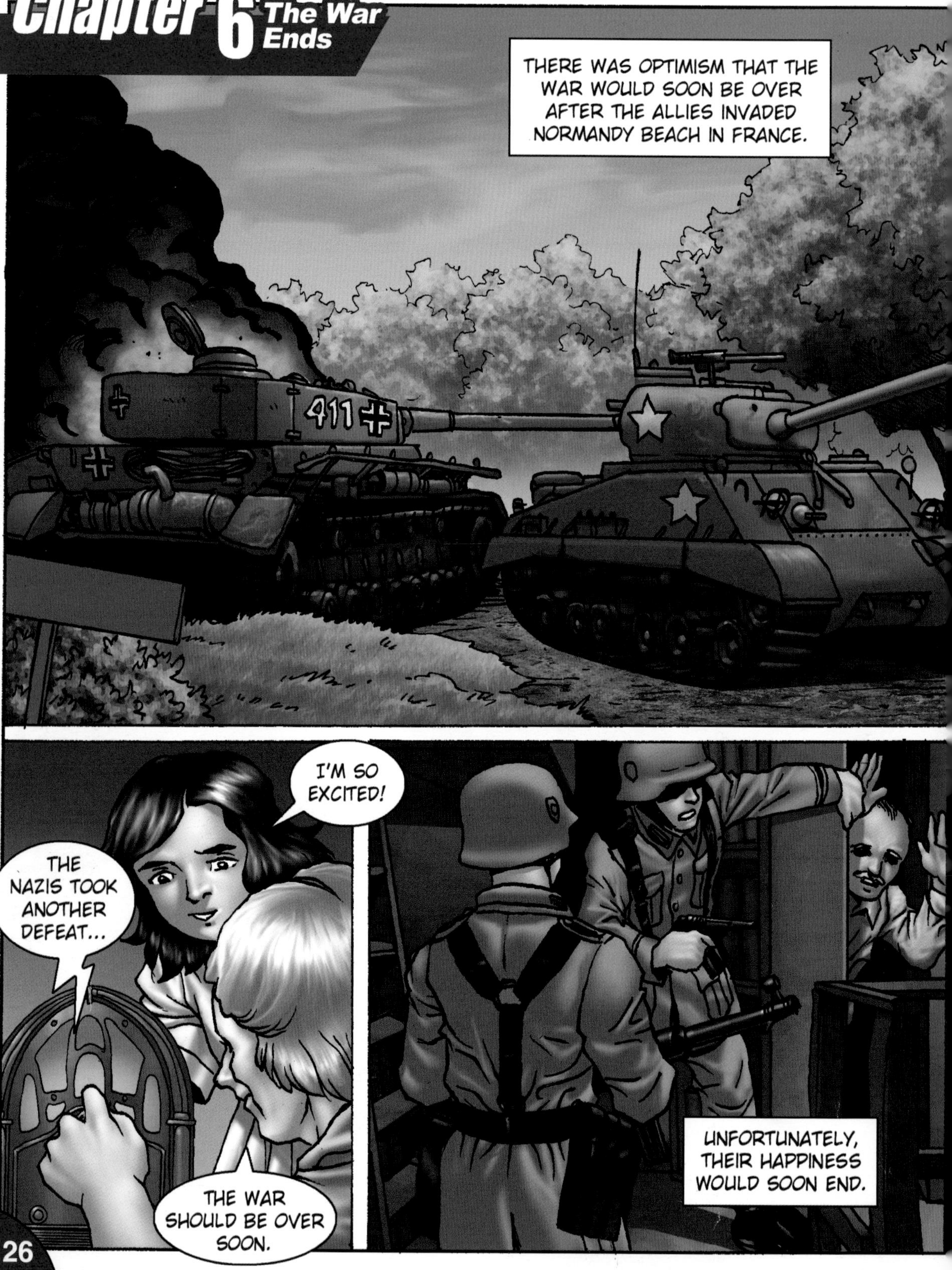
THERE WAS OPTIMISM THAT THE WAR WOULD SOON BE OVER AFTER THE ALLIES INVADED NORMANDY BEACH IN FRANCE.
411
I'M SO EXCITED!
THE NAZIS TOOK ANOTHER DEFEAT...
THE WAR SHOULD BE OVER SOON.
UNFORTUNATELY, THEIR HAPPINESS WOULD SOON END.

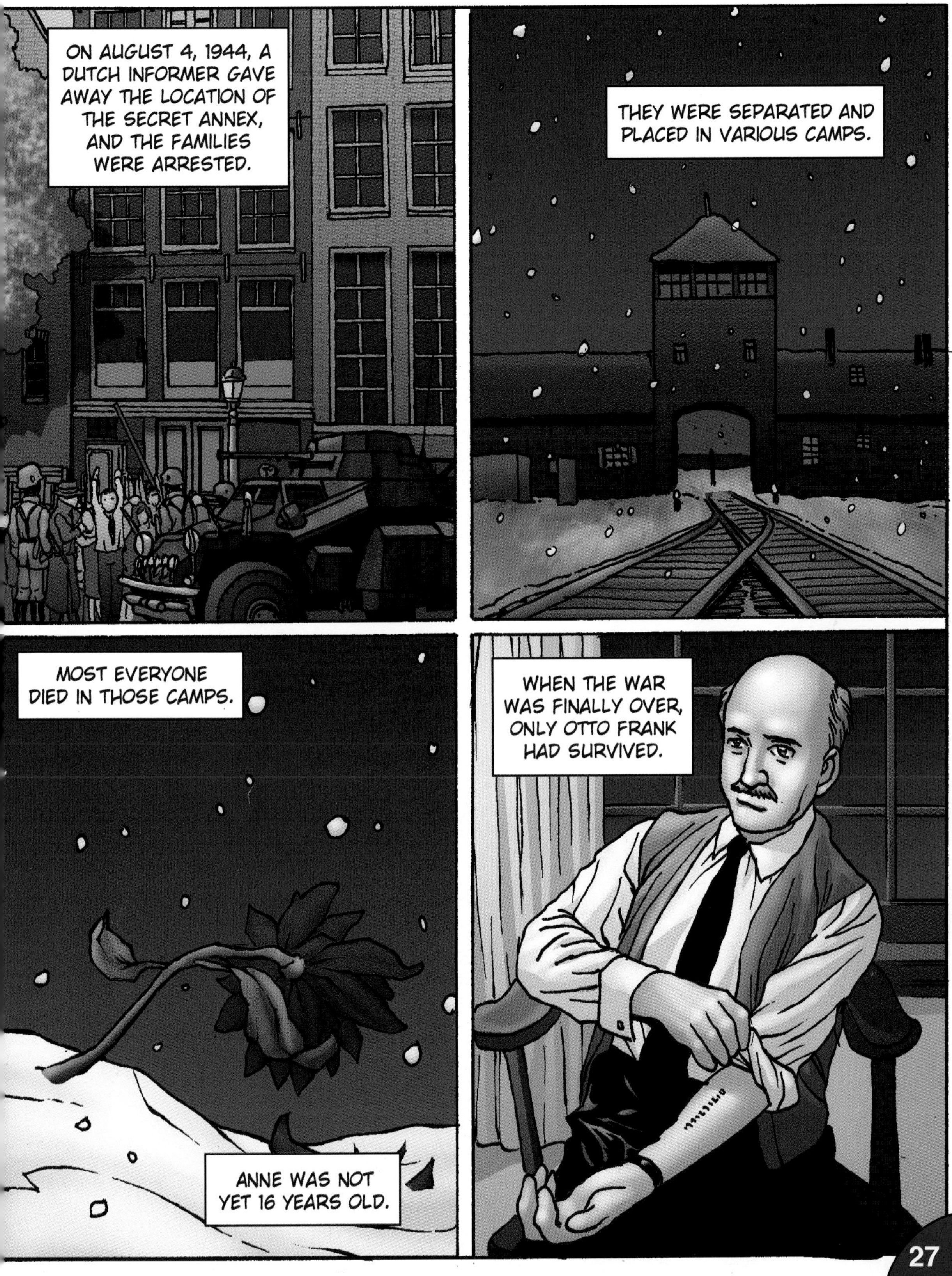
ON AUGUST 4, 1944, A DUTCH INFORMER GAVE AWAY THE LOCATION OF THE SECRET ANNEX, AND THE FAMILIES WERE ARRESTED.
THEY WERE SEPARATED AND PLACED IN VARIOUS CAMPS.
MOST EVERYONE DIED IN THOSE CAMPS.
ANNE WAS NOT YET 16 YEARS OLD.
WHEN THE WAR WAS FINALLY OVER, ONLY OTTO FRANK HAD SURVIVED.

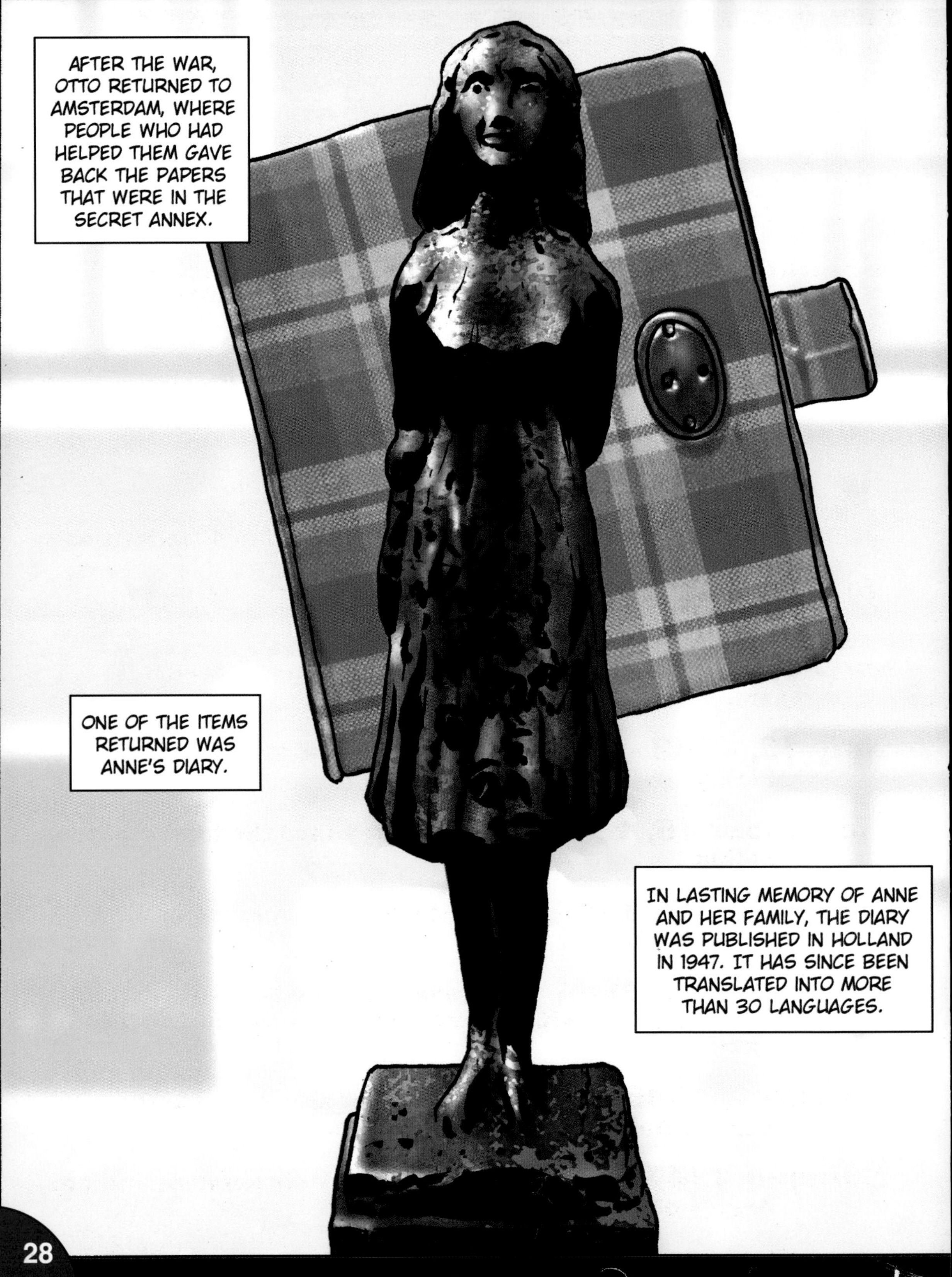
AFTER THE WAR, OTTO RETURNED TO AMSTERDAM, WHERE PEOPLE WHO HAD HELPED THEM GAVE BACK THE PAPERS THAT WERE IN THE SECRET ANNEX.
ONE OF THE ITEMS RETURNED WAS ANNE'S DIARY.
IN LASTING MEMORY OF ANNE AND HER FAMILY, THE DIARY WAS PUBLISHED IN HOLLAND IN 1947. IT HAS SINCE BEEN TRANSLATED INTO MORE THAN 30 LANGUAGES.

# Timeline

**June 12, 1929** - Anneliese Marie Frank (Anne) was born in Frankfurt, Germany.

**January 30, 1933** - Adolf Hitler was appointed Chancellor of Germany. Soon after, the Nazi Party declared a boycott of Jewish businesses.

**Summer 1933** - The Franks moved to the Netherlands because of Nazi oppression. Otto Frank established a business in Amsterdam.

**April 1940** - Germany invaded the Netherlands.

**June 12, 1942** - Anne received a diary for her 13th birthday.

**July 5, 1942** - Margot Frank received a notice to go to a labor camp.

**July 6, 1942** - The family went into hiding in a "secret annex."

**July 13, 1942** - The van Pels family joined the Franks in hiding.

**November 16, 1942** - Fritz Pfeffer joined the families in hiding.

**August 4, 1944** - The residents were discovered and arrested.

**September 3, 1944** - All members were sent to a labor camp in Auschwitz. Some were then moved to other camps.

**February, 1945** - Anne Frank and her sister died in the Bergen Belsen concentration camp.

**Summer 1947** - Anne's father was the only survivor and got Anne's diary published.

**Epstein, Rachel S.** *Anne Frank*. New York: Scholastic Library Publishing, 1998.

**Hurwitz, Johanna.** *Anne Frank: Life in Hiding*. New York: HarperCollins Publishers, 1999.

**Poole, Josephine.** *Anne Frank*. New York: Random House Children's Books, 2005.

**Woog, Adam.** *Anne Frank*. Michigan: Thomson Gale, 2004.

# Glossary

**allies** - people or countries that agree to help each other in times of need. During World War II Great Britain, France, the United States, and the Soviet Union were called the Allies.

**annex** - a building or structure that is added to an existing building.

**aspire** - to try to accomplish a particular goal.

**decree** - an official decision or order.

**deport** - to force someone who is not a citizen to leave the country.

**dictator** - a ruler with complete control who usually governs in a cruel or unfair way.

**infestation** - a large number of pests that cause trouble or harm.

**optimism** - an inclination to anticipate the best possible outcome.

# Web Sites

**To learn more about Anne Frank, visit ABDO Publishing Company on the World Wide Web at www.abdopublishing.com. Web sites about Frank are featured on our Book Links page. These links are routinely monitored and updated to provide the most current information available.**

# Index

## A
Aachen, Holland 9
Allies 26
Amsterdam, Holland 9, 28

## D
Denmark 10
diary 11, 12, 13, 14, 18, 20, 22, 25, 28

## E
education 11, 16, 25

## F
Frank, Edith 6, 9, 11, 14, 17, 19, 22, 25, 27
Frank, Margot 6, 9, 11, 14, 17, 19, 20, 22, 27
Frank, Otto 6, 9, 11, 14, 15, 16, 17, 19, 20, 22, 25, 27, 28
Frankfurt, Germany 6

## H
Hitler, Adolf 8, 9

## K
Kleiman 17

## N
Nazi Party 7, 8, 10, 11, 14, 18, 26
Norway 10

## P
Pfeffer, Fritz 17, 19, 27
Poland 10

## V
Van Pels family 15, 16, 17, 19, 20, 22, 23, 27
Versailles, Treaty of 7

## W
work camps 10, 14, 27
World War I 7